How To Develop the Mind
of Christ In You

by
Louise Brock

Harrison House
Tulsa, Oklahoma

How To Develop the Mind of Christ In You
ISBN 0-89274-787-0
Copyright © 1993, 1995 by Louise Brock
Faith Community Church
2551 W. Orange Grove Road
Tucson, Arizona 85741

Published by Harrison House, Inc.
P. O. Box 35035
Tulsa, Oklahoma 74153

Dedication

I lovingly dedicate this book to my precious Mother and Daddy. Ordained into the ministry over sixty years ago, they have established fourteen churches and reached thousands for the Lord Jesus Christ with their preaching.

They have been my "living epistles." I am following them as they follow Christ. Their faithfulness to Our Lord is a constant encouragement to me.

Contents

Contents

Acknowledgments

No book is ever the work of just one person, and this one is certainly no exception.

Thank you to Bea Olsen and Carlinda Budd for your transcriptions of the messages that served as the foundation for this book.

Thank you to my two sons, Bruce and Brian, who consistently encouraged me to persevere with this project.

Thank you to my Faith Community Church family in Tucson, Arizona, for your prayer support.

Thank you to Family Community Church of Sacramento, California, who gave me my first offering toward the publishing of this book.

And finally, thank you to Bruce and Christine Wingard, who took all the various pieces of this project and turned them into a book.

God bless you, one and all!

1
The Invitation

1
The Invitation

How badly do you want it?

In many areas of the Christian life the question above is the bottom line.

Are you willing to pay the price necessary to achieve what God has called you to do in the kingdom of God? Are you willing to come out of your comfort zone in order to be used of the Lord? So many of us have trudged along hoping things would get better and we would understand more of God's ways. Well, I want to tell you something — God doesn't work that way!

Dear heart, if you aren't willing to walk the way of the Lord, you had better bring along your own flashlight because the Lord reserves His light for those who walk in His ways. If you aren't willing to bring your thoughts into captivity to Christ and allow the Holy Spirit to develop the mind of Christ in you, then here is what will happen to you.

As times get tougher and your level of stress increases, your thinking will get muddier and muddier and your ability to discern things spiritually will diminish. Your decision-making faculties will come to depend almost entirely upon the wisdom of the world, and you will be left wide open to Satan's attacks.

Even now, almost on a daily basis, I encounter decisions, situations and people who make demands on resources I don't possess. I have to allow the wisdom that is from the Lord, the mind of Christ, to rise up in me and show me the way, give me the words to say or add to my strength. How about you?

When this teaching was first delivered, there was a prophecy given that bears on this point:

> *Indeed these are perilous times. These are last days, and they are perilous times. These are the days when seducing spirits and doctrines of demons are loosed upon us in hordes that we never believed possible before. These are the days when we must walk in the greatest discernment that we have ever walked in. Within each of you, I have placed My Holy Spirit which acts as a warning and a beacon, and you have the discerning within you to keep you from error. I have given you the Spirit of Truth Who now abides in you, and that anointing that rests in you will not let you go into error if you will listen to the anointing that abides.*

> *For the Spirit of Truth was sent for such a time as this: when those who come against you with their deceptive practices and with doctrines of devils, when those have come against you with new age philosophy and they have tried to coat it over with the doctrines of the Church. It is time for you to allow that Spirit of Truth and that simple operation of discernment to be very operative in your life.*

The operation of discernment is conducted by the mind of Christ under the power of the Holy Spirit. The Holy Spirit and the mind of Christ work together. You see, the Holy Spirit is a real person, not just a spiritual blob living inside you. He has to be able to communicate with you somehow. The reason you have the mind of Christ is because you have the Holy Spirit in you. Because He has that mind, therefore, so do you. It isn't that your mind has been replaced by the mind of Christ, but rather, that your mind is being renewed and retrained by the Holy Spirit, as you allow it, to flow and think in the same patterns He does.

You need the mind of Christ.

"Yes, Louise, but how do I get it?"

You already have it! Are you surprised? Don't be. The Word says that we have the mind of Christ. You received that gift when you were born again into the kingdom of His dear Son Jesus. **But we have the mind of Christ** (1 Cor. 2:16 NKJV).

Well, if the Bible says we have it, why don't we use it more often? That is a good question. Let's take a moment to answer that one before we go on.

It Must Be Developed

Developing the mind of Christ requires our cooperation with the Holy Spirit. The mind of Christ must be developed in us to be useful to us and to the Lord. When you were born, you had muscles, but they weren't too useful to you, were they? You possessed them, but couldn't use them. What happened? As you developed those muscles, you became stronger and more coordinated.

Well, the same thing happens with your mental "muscles," as it were. A baby learns that a spherical object is called a ball and a cube-like object is a block. So when you put a pyramid-shaped object in front of her, she tries to identify it as either a ball or a block because that is all she knows. There has to be additional mental development and experience before she can identify other shapes and move on to higher thoughts and concepts.

All truth is parallel, that is, if something is true in the natural realm, it will also be true in the spiritual arena. Therefore, if muscles and mental processes must be developed in the natural realm to be useful, then we can understand that the mind of Christ, God's gift to us at our spiritual birth, must also be developed if it is going to be of any use to us later on.

And that is what this book is all about —developing the mind of Christ in you.

Higher Thoughts — Higher Ways

In Isaiah 55 the prophet records the words of God:

> **For My thoughts are not your thoughts, nor are your ways My ways, says the Lord.**
>
> **For as the heavens are higher than the earth, so are My ways higher than your ways, and My thoughts than your thoughts.**
>
> Isaiah 55:8-9 NKJV

Now, on the surface, it seems we could forget ever understanding how God thinks, why He does things the way He does or how to pattern our ways after His. He seems to be a mystery Who is unsolvable to our puny little minds.

But what you must understand is that while our puny little minds cannot understand the mysteries of God, the mind of Christ can. Look at why Paul said God's grace was extended to him:

> **. . . to make all see what is the fellowship of the mystery, which from the beginning of the ages has been hidden in God who created all things through Jesus Christ;**
>
> **to the intent that now the manifold wisdom of God might be made known by the church to the principalities and powers in the heavenly places,**
>
> **according to the eternal purpose which He accomplished in Christ Jesus our Lord.**
>
> Ephesians 3:9-11 NKJV

Philippians 2:5 NKJV says it another way: **Let this mind be in you which was also in Christ Jesus.**

Paul could not have given this directive if it were not possible for us to have the mind of Christ. Colossians 1:9 NKJV adds to the body of evidence by stating:

14

For this reason we also, since the day we heard it, do not cease to pray for you, and to ask that you may be filled with the knowledge of His will in all wisdom and spiritual understanding.

Paul said he bowed his knees on our behalf that we might:

. . . be able to comprehend with all the saints what is the width and length and depth and height —

to know the love of Christ which passes knowledge; that you may be filled with all the fullness of God.
Ephesians 3:18-19 NKJV

Because you do indeed possess the mind of Christ, you can know the mysteries of God. You can indeed think like God thinks and pattern your ways after His ways, and you can do it in confidence. You can grow in understanding and develop this fabulous gift within you.

Our Invitation

But let's back up a minute and look at the beginning of the fifty-fifth chapter of Isaiah. There is something amazing there. It is an invitation, an invitation to an abundant life. Didn't Jesus tell us He came that we might have life and that more abundantly? Yes, He did. So let's look at this invitation and learn some powerful lessons for developing the mind of Christ.

Ho! Everyone who thirsts, come to the waters; and you who have no money, come, buy and eat. Yes, come, buy wine and milk without money and without price.
Isaiah 55:1 NKJV

This invitation was made by Father God to His people in exile in Babylon. He is summoning them to remove themselves from Babylonian influences in order that they may be partakers in the covenant blessings. This is the same summons that the Father extends to us.

We, too, must remove ourselves from the world's influences and its way of thinking, as well as from its patterns and ways of living, in order to participate in our Heavenly Father's covenant of blessings.

The mind of Christ is one of our covenant blessings, but few of us ever develop the use of it sufficiently for it to have any impact on our daily lives.

In the very near future that is going to have to change, not only for you but for the Church as a whole.

I am telling you, the things of this world do not satisfy the inner longing. Why? Because our inner being, our spirit man, craves that which is from the Father God — spiritual food. Now, if you think about it, that makes perfect sense. Your spiritual man needs spiritual food just as your natural man needs natural food.

Those who are satisfied with the world right now, those who are already so caught up in their worldly situations, those who depend upon the merit of the works of their own hands to bring them some sort of righteousness — they don't have any thirst at all for the things of God.

The invitation is for the thirsty.

I speak every week with people who have known God at one time, who were once very close to Him, who used to hunger and thirst after Him; but today they couldn't care less about the things of God. They have lost their thirst. Do you know why? They have lost their saltiness. Salt creates a thirst for water. We make the world thirsty. We are salt to the world because the Word of God lives and abides in us. The life of God, the Word of God and the love of God all abide in us, making us salty to the world and to each other and creating a spiritual thirst. But I talk to people all the time who have lost their spiritual saltiness.

How many of you remember those times of revival or when you were first born again or when you got a healing?

You couldn't wait to get to church! But now it is an effort. What has happened? Check your salt shaker.

Now the fires of persecution are coming to the Church again, and it won't be like a lot of people think. It is going to drive the unsalted, the lukewarm and the convenient Christians right back to church.

Ever since I have been meditating on and studying Isaiah 55, I have been asking the Father to make me, the ministry and the leadership of the church so salty that men and women will be driven to the living waters of Jesus Christ to have their thirst slaked.

If you want the things of God, you can have them. The choice is yours. The question is — how badly do you want them? Jesus said the one who hungered and thirsted after righteousness would be filled. How thirsty are you?

The Water of Life

In John's gospel Jesus meets the Samaritan woman at the well, and He tells her that the water He gives . . . **will become in him a fountain of water springing up into everlasting life** (John 4:14 NKJV). The Bible is alive with types, illustrations and outright statements about Jesus being the source of the waters of life. When the Lord chose a sacrament to symbolize our becoming one with Him, He chose total immersion in water. Water baptism is, perhaps, the single most pointed reference to Jesus being the water of life.

Isn't it interesting, then, that in the invitation in Isaiah 55:1 we are invited to come to the waters? Follow this carefully now, and you will see the divine cycle of the flow of the life of Jesus through us to the world, a flow that edifies at the same time. Let me explain.

First, we received the life of Jesus when we heard the Word and believed on Him in our hearts and confessed

Him before men. Then, because of the Word which was sown in our hearts, we became spiritually salty. This saltiness not only attracted others who were thirsting after life, but it served to augment our own thirst. We became thirsty for more of God. This brought us back to the waters of life in Jesus to satisfy our thirst which, in turn, increased the level of the flow of Jesus' life through us, making us even saltier. And so the cycle continues during all our lives until we are conformed to the image of Jesus.

Where is our starting point? Where do we come first? We come to the waters — to Jesus, the fountain of living water. It is interesting to note that in Bible days *coming to the waters* was a term used to mean "coming to the city fountains." **If any man thirst**, He said in John, chapter seven, verse thirty-seven, **let him come unto me, and drink.**

Then Jesus turned right around and said to us, the Body of Christ-to-be, **He who believes in Me, as the Scripture has said, out of his heart will flow rivers of living water** (John 7:38 NKJV). The same waters that flowed from Jesus Christ can now flow from you. People can come to you and have their thirst slaked.

Beware of Bitter Water

Now, let me ask you a question. Why do you think satanism, humanism and New Age are so popular? It is because people have a spiritual thirst that must be satisfied. However, they are filling that spiritual gap with bitter water from the world of darkness. People want some spiritual connection so badly that they will even accept spiritual counterfeits. According to some reports these counterfeits are growing faster than the Church is right now.

Our local newspaper recently listed some statistics. The headline read, "New Age Movement Has Old-Time

Religion Camp Nervous." It told about the hordes of people who are coming into channeling, into the New Age movement and into transcendental meditation. Why? Because it is spiritual. And the fact that it is from the realm of darkness rather than the realm of light doesn't matter to them. And Satan, of course, to excite them further, is obliging them and giving them supernatural experiences.

What is even worse, and this really disturbs me as I travel around the country, I see people trying to mix authentic Christianity and New Age junk. Did you know that we have Holy Spirit-filled people, praying people, people in charismatic churches who are trying to mix the two? I just recently got through correcting someone — strongly — on the way she was praying. She was praying witchcraft!

I am here to tell you that if you start mixing that junk in with the power of the Holy Spirit, you will be in worse shape than somebody who never knew to do good, and it won't take long to get you there. Worse yet, your inner craving for the things of God will still not be satisfied.

You can't mix the two. It is like mixing oil and water. You cannot take the supernatural of the realm of darkness and the supernatural of the realm of light and mix them together.

While we are on the subject, I want you to be aware of another false teaching going around since the New Age Movement became popular: that light and darkness are both parts of the same supernatural dimension, opposite sides of the same coin, so to speak. That is a lie spawned in the slime of the pit of hell.

Look at the basic facts. The kingdom of darkness is, in actuality, only a principality which is limited to one planet, Earth. And even on Earth, Satan is further limited to only where the sons and daughters of the Most High God permit him to continue to operate. Satan's domain is out of his absolute control.

By contrast, the kingdom of God is the entire universe, every planet, including the domain of Satan, as God's children rise to their position of rulership by taking authority over Satan in the name of Jesus. For comparison's sake we might say that Satan's domain is the dark side of a dirty penny while God's kingdom is the entire mint full of bright, shiny silver dollars.

A Starting Point

Have you decided you want the Holy Spirit to rise and live big in you so you will be able to correctly discern the operation of the mind of Christ in your life? Then these three points are a starting place for your development of the mind of Christ in you:

1. *Make sure you are grounded in the Word.* In the areas of your special concern, make sure you know what the Word says. In other words, know what God has to say about whatever it is you are dealing with. If you don't, stop! Take the time to find out what the Bible says before you go one step further.

2. *Make sure you have listened to the Holy Spirit for His counsel and teaching concerning whatever you are dealing with.* In other words, don't rely solely on your own wisdom. Get used to checking in with the Holy Spirit for His input on a regular basis.

3. *Most important of all, take the time to pray in the Holy Spirit.* No, take more time than that. Praying in tongues will lift you up above perilous times, up above seducing spirits and up above the seduction of the world. In other words, stay full of the Holy Spirit, and you will be edified. This will also make the first two items in this short list easier as well.

Dear one, you must learn to stay in tune with the Holy Spirit. He is the Spirit of Truth. He is the Protector of the Church. (That is you!) He is the One Who hedges His Church about, and He is the One Who brings you into that higher place where you can hear His higher thoughts.

God's higher thoughts are still being revealed to His Church, and you will learn them as you walk in and listen to the Holy Spirit. You will receive them as you pray in the Spirit, and you will learn to trust them as you move in the Spirit.

There is no substitute for this path. Every servant of the Lord must walk this way. You are not about to be the first exception. This plan has existed since before the foundations of the earth, and we must conform to His ways, not demand that He conform to ours.

In the same prophecy I quoted to you earlier, the Lord also said,

I am always willing to impart to you My higher thoughts. I have not thought them to hide them and to make it very difficult for you to find. I have made My higher thoughts pure revelation. The only price that you have to pay is to literally come and submit yourself and do those things — be thirsty, come without money, just come with time and effort into My presence, waiting carefully there in My presence — and I will reveal, through the power of revelation, these higher thoughts to you.

These thoughts will save you from making serious mistakes in some decision that you are facing. These higher thoughts will bring you into that realm where you will not allow the pressure and the stress of this world to force you into corners where you've got to make decisions in a hurry concerning your finances.

These higher thoughts that I am bringing to you as you wait in My presence are yours simply for the waiting.

21

*You come and you buy them with your presence and the
attitude of your heart. I am so eager to reveal My higher
thoughts and higher ways, and the directions that you
have been praying for, but you don't fill yourself long
enough in My presence for Me to reveal these higher
places and these higher thoughts to you and the way to
move into these higher thoughts.*

Take a moment to reread the prophecy I have just
quoted and the three beginning steps.

Aren't you struck with the numerous references to
time? Each of the three beginning steps requires a
dedication of time, a commitment to make time for an
activity that is a priority in the way we run our lives. Not
only that, but the prophecy over and over again emphasizes
the need for time spent in the Lord's presence.

How often, when we see a man or woman of God who
is walking closer to the Lord or perhaps doing more for
Him than we are, do we think, "Boy, I wish I could do that."
Well, you can! The Lord has extended the invitation. Are
you thirsty enough? Are you hungry enough? Is it worth it
to you to spend the time in His presence required to obtain
it?

Only you can answer that question. If your answer is
yes, then read on. If it is no, then I suggest you put this book
down until you can honestly answer yes because you will
never move into the deeper things of God, you will never
move up to the higher thoughts and ways of God and you
will never develop the mind of Christ in you until you are
willing to take the time it requires.

Are you going on? I hope so.

2
The Challenge

2

The Challenge

You are going to have to change your life.

That is right, dear one. Doesn't it stand to reason that if you change your mind, you will have to change your life as a result? If you are not willing to change your life, then you are just fooling yourself. Once you change your mind, how you think will be different. How you view people will be different. How you react to things, events and circumstances will be different. And, of course, how you feel about all of this will change.

Are you surprised? Don't be, and don't be discouraged either. You won't have to do it all on your own, nor will you have to do it all in your own strength. The Holy Spirit is the One Who is going to affect the changes. Your job is to allow Him to do His work and cooperate with Him when He does. Sounds simple, doesn't it? It is. But it isn't easy. After all, you have been the way you are for some time now, haven't you? And, like most people, even though there are things about you and your life that you don't like, you are very resistant to change. Yet, change has been happening to you all your life long — some good, some bad, but there has always been change. There always will be.

The Hard Part

The challenge is to be in control of that change in such a way that it conforms to the Word of God for your life.

Let's not beat around the bush. Here it is. In order to develop the mind of Christ in you, you will have to be able to handle the challenge of change in your life, and in order to handle that change, you will need to do four things:

1. *Be willing to put your natural mind aside.*

2. *Make the sacrifice to renew your mind.*

3. *Don't allow yourself to be deceived, even by yourself.*

4. *Be disciplined in prayer and the Word.*

I suppose I could have put this list at the end of the chapter as a summary, but I think you might just as well know what you are up against from the beginning. After all, I said it was a challenge, didn't I?

These things might look impossible to you at this point. They are not. You might understand the words but not have any real practical understanding of what is involved in doing each of these four things. Don't worry.

A Common Thread

I have good news for you. There is a common thread that runs through all four aspects of the challenge. If you remember that thread, then, as a rudder on a ship, it will keep you pointed in the right direction through the rough waters that may lie ahead.

Now, don't let the prospect of rough water scare you. Surely you know, don't you, that even if you don't respond to the challenge of developing the mind of Christ in you, you will have rough sailing at certain points anyway? Life is full of challenges. This challenge of rough seas is simply one we have picked to answer on purpose, together.

The common thread is a principle: you can't develop the mind of Christ in you without developing your relationship with the Holy Spirit because that is where the mind of Christ is — in the Holy Spirit. You build yourself up, you change yourself, you grow spiritually by deliberately developing the communion between you and the Holy Spirit, Who is alive in you.

But remember — you can't develop the mind of Christ by developing your own mind, only by renewing it to the things of the Holy Spirit. Simply put, the flesh can't accomplish the work of the Spirit, not even in you.

Understand, dear one, that there is more to this than just will power. Make no mistake about it, your will is very involved, and you will be more disciplined when we are done, but we have to go beyond our own strength to His strength.

Come, Buy and Eat

How many of you can't wait to get into the Word every morning or every evening? How many of you can't wait to get into the presence of God? You wake up praying in the Spirit or singing a song to Him or from Him. You just can't wait to feel His sweet presence, first thing.

I will tell you what — there are times when I have to take myself by the scruff of my neck, sit myself down and make myself read the Word. I don't count it all joy every day either. It is a discipline I make myself do, and it is work. But you know what I have found out? The more I discipline myself, the more I want to be in the Word and in His presence and the more joyous the time becomes. Your flesh will respond to the leadership of your spirit.

The Lord knows how we are built; He made us. He knows that the more involved we become in anything we do, the better we become at it and the easier it is for us to do.

Therefore, it follows that the key here (in trying to discipline the flesh) is to do more than just drink of the water of life but to buy and eat also. We are to buy (ownership) and to eat (to make it a part of ourself, to consume it and be nurtured by it) the wine of the Holy Spirit and the milk of the Word. Great meat eater that you may be, remember, as the old commercial used to say, "You never outgrow your need for milk."

Let's return to our foundation Scripture for this study. There is something more there we need to understand:

> **Ho! Everyone who thirsts, come to the waters; and you who have no money, come, buy and eat. Yes, come, buy wine and milk without money and without price.**
>
> **Why do you spend money for what is not bread, and your wages for what does not satisfy?**
>
> Isaiah 55:1-2 NKJV

Now, notice, verse one says, **Come and buy wine and milk,** but the invitation is addressed to those who have no money. You don't have to be especially bright to figure out that if something is bought, as opposed to given, there has to be a price paid somewhere along the line. Where is the price paid here? Jesus paid that price. By His death and resurrection He has spent the coin of His blood to purchase covenant rights that we are learning to exercise.

Therefore, we do not need any medium of exchange to obtain the wine and milk mentioned in verse one. No quibbling about price, no quibbling about terms. But the wine and the milk are not free. Remember, Jesus paid for them for us. What are we required to do in order to receive them?

We will talk about what the wine and the milk represent in a moment, but first, let's address the issue of buying without any money.

In biblical times, if the master of a house agreed to buy some fruit daily from a certain merchant, that merchant would likely see the master's servant at his fruit stand every morning. The fruit merchant would give the servant the fruit and charge it to the master's account. The servant did the buying, but the master paid the price. So it is with us.

But to complete the transaction, there are two things the servant must do. First, he must wait in the presence of the merchant for his master's fruit, and second, the servant must have a good attitude while waiting, or it will cost his master the goodwill of the merchant.

These higher thoughts that flow from the mind of Christ because of the presence of the Holy Spirit within you are yours simply for the waiting. You come and "buy" them with your presence and the attitude of your heart. God is eager to reveal His higher thoughts and higher ways and the direction for which you have been praying. But, most of the time, you don't fill yourself in His presence long enough for Him to reveal these higher thoughts to you, much less the way to move into and flow with these higher thoughts.

Our natural man wants to come on the basis of our own works, our own coin. Impossible. God operates by grace. Who has first given God anything that He might be paid back? You can't pay God back. With what would you pay Him? All you or I can bring to Him is our worthlessness, our own self-righteousness, which is as filthy rags. You can't pay God back because it is a grace gift. He loved you first. Because of His love and your response to it, you have entered into a covenant of grace.

More than just buy, we are also commanded to eat. The Father is saying, in effect, do more than just own his provision; you are to "eat" them until they become part of you. That which we eat is more ours than that which we merely buy.

Why do you spend money for what is not bread, and your wages for what does not satisfy? the Lord asks in Isaiah 55:2 NKJV. We are pressed to receive His invitation. The second half of verse two begins: **Hearken diligently unto me** (KJV) **or Listen carefully to Me** (NKJV).

Over and over as I have studied this, in those first three verses there is an intensity in God's voice. It is as if between the lines He is saying, "Listen to what I'm saying; hearken to my Word; listen; let it get into you! I'm giving you all these proposals. Why do you spend your money for that which is not bread when with Me you can have wine and milk without money?"

We can all agree that, on the surface, it doesn't make any sense to be offered so much and to settle for so little. So why do we do it? Because the thinking of the world, the lower thoughts of this age, have conditioned us to think like that.

I know *you* never would, but some people think: "If I had all my bills paid, and I was out of debt, and I had a new car and a bigger house, maybe even paid for, and I had a little money in the bank, then I would be satisfied." That is a cheap lie! If you believe that lie, you have sold yourself far short of the blessings the Lord has for you. The world says those things will satisfy you, but the people who have all that, and more, are no more satisfied than you are, particularly the Christians.

The things of this world do not satisfy the inner longing. Why? Because our inner being craves that which is from our Heavenly Father — spiritual food.

You not only have to "buy" it by waiting in His presence with the attitude of a willing heart, but you have to "eat" it. You must eat the spiritual food the Father feeds you. And, just as with natural food, that takes time. We need to be nourished by spiritual food every bit as much as our bodies need natural food.

Water, Wine and Milk

There were three basics in every Judean home —water, wine and milk. These things were always there.

Therefore, it is no accident that these three items were chosen for the Father's invitation in Isaiah 55:1-2. We have already seen that the water spoken of is the water of life in Christ Jesus, but what of the wine and the milk?

Wine has at least two symbolic interpretations in Scripture. The first is as the blood of Christ, and the second is as a type of the Holy Spirit. It is also a symbol for joy — joy in the Spirit. Wine is the product of the fruit of the vine. The vine produces grapes which produce wine. Wine is the usable end product of fruitfulness. So it is with us. The Holy Spirit is the end product of God's gift, Jesus, to the creation He loves, man. We are called to partake of the Spirit and His fruit in our lives.

Where the Holy Spirit is concerned, we are:

   *convicted by Him

   *indwelt by Him

   *filled by Him

   *baptized in Him

   *taught by Him

   *and led by Him

The Holy Spirit is a person, not a fuzzy blob. The above list is a big job. It is nothing we could even remotely do for ourselves, yet it is an ongoing requirement for living the fulfilled Christian life. Come and buy. Come and eat. Come and be satisfied by the work and the fruit of the Holy Spirit in your life. Then you can minister His love to others.

Milk has some interesting symbolism in Scripture as well; however, in every reference to it, one characteristic of milk is always present —nourishment. Milk always represents something which gives nourishment. Perhaps, as Paul wrote in Hebrews 5:12, it refers to a state of spiritual development that cannot receive the strong meat of the

Word, but only the nourishment of milk, of simple things, first things.

> **For though by this time you ought to be teachers, you need someone to teach you again the first principles of the oracles of God; and you have come to need milk and not solid food.**
>
> Hebrews 5:12 NKJV

Or perhaps it refers to the much needed **pure milk of the word** as Peter referred to it in 1 Peter 2:2 NKJV: **as newborn babes, desire the pure milk of the word, that you may grow thereby.**

In either case, it is clear that milk refers to the Word of God. We cannot neglect our spiritual feedings. We won't grow properly. How could we? It is always tempting to believe that we have reached the state of spiritual maturity where we no longer need the milk of the Word, but rather, that we are ready for real meat.

I will tell you what — if the mind of Christ has yet to be developed in you, then you still need your milk. Are you drinking the Word several times a day?

Dear one, three things are needful for a full life in Jesus, and you are invited to come and freely partake of all of them:

1. *The water*, which is the new life in Jesus;

2. *The wine*, which is the joy and leadership of the Holy Spirit;

3. *The milk*, which is the nourishment of the Word.

All three are necessary. All three are free. All three were bought and paid for by the blood of Jesus. Come, buy and eat. Come and be satisfied.

3
Higher Thoughts — Part 1

3

Higher Thoughts—Part I

3
Higher Thoughts
Part 1

You are thinking too low.

 You are thinking too short.

  You are thinking too small.

However you say it, the fact remains that God's thoughts are higher than ours. What Paul calls the "mind of Christ" in the New Testament is referred to as God's "higher thoughts" in the Old Testament. As we develop the mind of Christ in us, we begin moving into that realm of God's higher thoughts.

As long as we are in this body, on this earth, we are going to have to be renewing our minds continually. We are going to have to be putting our natural minds under subjection to our spirit and tuning into the mind of Christ, the higher thoughts of God.

Follow with me for just a moment. When someone is able to predict how another person is going to act in a given situation — say you and your spouse, for example — it is almost always because you know how your spouse thinks. And because you know how they think, you can fairly accurately predict how they will respond. But, how did you learn how they think? You learned by observing and coming to know their ways in countless other similar situations, didn't you?

In fact, the closer in relationship you are to the person you are getting to know, the more accurate your predictions of their behavior will be. Right?

You see, without a relationship with that person, it would have been impossible for you to predict accurately how they would respond. The best you could do would be to observe their acts and make educated guesses. A person's ways are an outward expression of their motivations, priorities, styles, options and goals — all the inner "stuff" our personality and our character are made of. And all that cannot be fully known outside of a relationship with that person.

Once you develop your relationship with God and you begin to know His ways, then you can think His higher thoughts in those situations where you have learned His ways.

But getting that close to God can be scary. Some would rather hold themselves at a distance and simply observe, "That is all, thank you very much." Psalm 103:7 NKJV says, **He made known His ways to Moses, His acts to the children of Israel.** Why the difference?

Moses and the People

Moses was a man who stood in the presence of God. He was not afraid to go to the top of the mountain and get into God's presence, face to face, for as many days as it took. For that, God revealed His ways to Moses. Do you know what that was? Revelation in its purest form. Moses would then come down and tell the children of Israel what God had said to him because they said, "Moses, we don't want to hear God's voice." (Ex. 20:18,19.)

God intended for every child of Israel to know His ways. He didn't want to work through an intermediary. God wanted to call them all to the top of the mountain and speak to each of them through revelation. His desire was for every Israelite to come into the same marvelous, holy presence Moses had. God is no respecter of persons. God loved the loneliest little member of the tribe of Ephraim as much as he loved Moses. He desired for every one of His kids, including you, to come into His presence — into the living, vibrant presence of Almighty God.

But the children of Israel made an historic decision when Moses came down the mountain and invited them all to come up and meet God as he had. They saw the manifestation of the power and presence of God on the mountain: The mountain shuddered and shook and smoked, and there was fire. It sounded like a freight train going through everybody's head. And their reaction was, "That is God?" Moses said, "That is God." The people said, "Then we don't we want to go up there. We are about as close as we want to get. We don't think we want to smell like smoke. We don't think we want to walk in that kind of glory — because it is scary." (Ex. 20:18-21.)

I am sure Moses wanted to turn them all around and march them right up there to face God, but they wouldn't do it. As a result, Moses ended up knowing God's ways, and the children of Israel only saw His acts. Moses moved by revelation, but they moved only by observation. They stood on the sidelines all through the wilderness and watched God's acts; Moses knew how He was going to act.

They watched God roll back the waters of the Red Sea, and they watched Pharaoh's army drown. They watched the smoke, and they watched the glory of God on the mountain. They watched the manna delivered to them day after day. They looked up and saw the cloud that led them by day and shaded them. They were warmed by the pillar of fire, that great gigantic jet stream of flame that hovered over the camp by night.

They stood on the sidelines for forty years and watched their clothes never wear out. They watched their shoes never get thin, and they watched themselves staying healthy, those who believed God, for none of the diseases of the Egyptians had come with them. They saw God's acts, but they never learned His ways.

If they had known God's ways, they would not have stood on the sidelines when it was time to take Canaan. They wouldn't have stood on the sidelines when the spies came back with ten bad reports and two good ones. They were led by their natural minds and by observation. They never moved into revelation. Moses moved into revelation, and as a result, he knew God's ways.

It is clear from reading Scripture that God's original plan for the Israelites was that they should all be priests, a nation of priests operating in His authority and power. And it would have happened right then if the people had gone up the mountain when Moses directed them. But they refused. So instead, God established one tribe, the tribe of Levi, as His priests. They became the intermediaries between God and His people.

But God's higher thoughts were much bigger than Israel's. God's plan included not just Israel but all nations. He was calling Israel to become His nation of priests to win an entire world back to Him, and they missed it.

Look in Revelation 5:10 and see the Bible's final statement about God's plan concerning the role of His children: **And [You] have made us kings and priests to our God.** We, the Church of Jesus, have been given what was to have been Israel's role thousands of years ago.

God's Plan and You

I asked my congregation a question some time back: "How many of you have made so many mistakes in the last three or four years that you know it is now time for you to hook into God's higher thoughts?" I couldn't count the raised hands. How about you? Would you like to live tapping into God's higher thoughts to avoid many mistakes you could be making in life? Would you like to get to the place where Satan can't get a foothold in you? God has a plan for you to do just that.

However, before that plan can be implemented, before you can walk so closely in the Spirit and be led completely by Him, there is yet another work that must be done in one or more areas of your life. You probably already know what that area is.

We all know people who keep facing the same obstacles in their lives over and over. The same strongholds or the same besetting sin plagues them repeatedly. It is as though they go around and around the same old stump. They chip and hack at it around the edges, but they never get in and pull the thing out by the root. Their victory in the spirit is never complete, never final, because they won't put forth the diligence, the effort and the faith to pull down that stronghold over their lives.

They are the same folks who will take a couple of aspirins for a headache because they haven't got time to stand in faith for their healing. Then they wonder why they can't get healed when something serious comes along. Every time God allowed some small test to develop their faith, they played hooky. They are undeveloped in knowing God's ways.

Now, be honest with yourself. Are you in the same condition?

Maybe you will have a small victory now and then as you go around that old stump of sin, rebellion or stubbornness in your life, and you will rejoice for a little while. You may even make a few solid cuts into it and think, "Well, the Holy Ghost is really going to dig it out this time." Then what happens? It is just a matter of weeks, or even days, until that thing is in control of your life again.

Don't get me wrong. I would love to dig your stump out for you. I would love to pray and fast and intercede and say to your stump, "Be removed!" But I can't! I can't read the Word *for* you. I can't pray in the Spirit *for* you. I cannot live spiritually *for* you. You must do it *for* yourself.

The kingdom of God does not operate as a representative form of government. God desires that each of us personally be led by His Spirit to do the work He has ordained for us to accomplish. To do that, we each must have a deep enough personal relationship with Him to know His ways and think His higher thoughts.

You say, "Well, it is sure easy for you. You are a minister, but I work in the world." Baloney! It takes the same amount of diligence for me as it does for you. I don't have fewer battles to fight. All that my place in the Body of Christ does for me is make me a bigger target for the Devil. My battles may be in different areas than yours, but they are just as tough as yours. I assure you.

I have to deal with bad attitudes in ministers and other people just as you do. I have to deal with sharks in the business world just as you do. I have to deal with all kinds of garbage all the time, and I want to tell you, if I didn't pay the price for the water and the wine and the milk, I would be in exactly the same boat that some of you are.

Are you bragging, Louise? You bet I am! I am bragging on Jesus, on the Holy Spirit alive in me, from Whom I draw on the mind of Christ and God's higher thoughts — thoughts He willingly shares with me.

Discipline has become a dirty word in our generation. We hate to do it, but there are no short cuts. The price of spiritual power is your diligence to come daily into His presence and receive from Him. Of course, you have to act on what you receive, or it will do you no good. Five minutes of revelation put to good use can do more for you than fifty years of observation or a lifetime of hard work.

I will tell you something. You can work your fingers to the bone, and all you will have is bony fingers and nothing else. You can do all those things the world tells you to do to be successful and still be empty and hurting inside. I am talking to believers now. Some of the most hurting people I know are those who have great amounts of leisure time and money, those who are the busiest in their church. However, because they have no personal relationship with Jesus, their spiritual tank gurgles around empty most of the time instead of being full to overflowing, as God desires.

Listen, Listen, Listen

In the book of Isaiah the prophet records the words of the Lord saying,

> Listen carefully to Me, and eat what is good, and let your soul delight itself in abundance.
>
> Incline your ear, and come to Me. Hear, and your soul shall live.
>
> Isaiah 55:2b-3a NKJV

Three times the prophet echoes the higher thoughts of God. Three times he emphasizes that we are to pay attention to the Word of the Lord and that it is to our great benefit to do so. We will look at each of those prophetic admonitions in a moment. If we want to get hooked into the higher thoughts of God and have the mind of Christ operational in our lives, it is important for us to understand exactly what the Lord is saying here and in the following verses.

Understand, these verses are addressed mainly to your soul. They may have a lot of application to the spirit, but for the most part they are addressed to your soul because your soul is where your emotions are. Your soul is where your desires are. The soul realm is where you have to battle all the time between the natural, or carnal, and the supernatural.

Paul said in the last days the battle would be for the minds of the believers. (2 Thess. 2:2 AMP.) Your soul is where your mind is. Mind, will, emotions, intellect and personality — they are all part of your soul.

Let me say something again. It is important. It is in your soul realm where you have to battle all the time between the natural and the supernatural. You see, the minute that you were born again your spirit was reborn. Jesus Christ made you a brand new spirit in His image. (2 Cor. 3:18 AMP.) Old things passed away; all things became new, and you became a brand new creature who had never existed before in your spirit. (2 Cor. 5:17.)

Your soul, however, is being renewed day by day. It is progressive. Salvation was instantaneous for your spirit, but it is progressive for your soul! As for your body, well, you have a wonderful, glorified body laid to your account in heaven, waiting for you either through rapture or the grave through resurrection. But your soul — that is your project for as long as you are alive.

It begins with your listening. And not just listening like you commonly think of it. There are three steps to truly listening:

   1. Listen

      2. Incline your ear

      3. Hear

Listen. Listen fully, completely, alertly, actively, totally, openly and without prejudice, without the filter of your traditions, without malice toward another, without discounting what you hear because of your fears and hurts, without judging the word on the basis of your personal experience and with the full realization that the Word of God is the supreme and perfect authority in the universe, and concerning it, there is no appeal. It is right; everything else is less.

Incline your ear. There must be a readiness to hear the Word of the Lord present in our lives. I have several friends whose judgment I truly trust, and whenever we are in a group discussion, I find myself inclining my ear to what they have to say. There is an eagerness to hear from them. It is like my receiver is tuned to their frequency. They come through louder and clearer than others.

That is the way we are to be with the Lord, if we really want to hear. Our hearts should be leaning towards Him, waiting for Him to speak.

Since I have learned to incline my ear, I am amazed at the people and situations the Lord uses to speak to me. In the middle of an ordinary conversation, a sentence or thought will stand out as though in bold print. "That is Me," the Lord will say by His Spirit, and I know I have heard Him, and I can trust what I hear. I must have missed literally thousands of opportunities to be led by the Spirit before I learned how important it was to keep the ear of my heart inclined toward God's voice.

In fact, to illustrate how important inclining your ear is to knowing the heart of God, if you remove the first and last letters of the word *heart*, you find what is at the center of the heart — the *ear*!

Hear. Oh, how important this aspect of listening is. It means to fully receive and understand. Understanding is absolutely necessary to building the confidence and hope within you that is foundational to acting in faith. Without understanding what you incline your ear to and listen to, you can't act in faith. You will act only in presumption.

Now look at the rewards for listening, inclining your ear and hearing.

For the listener the reward is learning what is good and receiving the abundant fruit thereof.

For the ones who incline their ears to the Lord, they will draw ever closer to Him. And for the ones who hear with understanding, the reward is life, a reviving of their spiritual life, at the highest dimension.

For all three there is a covenant that comes into play, the covenant based on the everlasting mercies of God.

The Sure Mercies of David

Your soul is the part of you that needs a revival, and your soul will be revived according to what you are hearing from the Father. But if you won't take time to listen to Him, you will be in big trouble. Why? Because all you will have to depend on is you and your wisdom.

Your spirit was instantly and totally reborn; however, your soul goes through being up one day and down the next. Get your soul in line with your spirit, which is indwelt by the Holy Spirit of God, so that you can function in the confidence of your covenant.

In Isaiah 55:3 we find the reward for those who listen, incline their ears and hear with understanding — the everlasting covenant of the sure mercies of David. The everlasting covenant promised to David is none other than a prophetic reference to the new covenant. Actually, it is a dual reference, both to the covenant of David and to the new covenant which was embodied in Jesus, King David's greater son.

In effect, God is saying, "If you will listen, your soul will revive, and I will make you an everlasting covenant. Even the sure mercy I promised to David, I will now promise to you. For you this covenant is the final basis for the revival, renewal and restoration of your souls. This new covenant is based not on laws, nor on justice, but upon the mercies (good will, love, compassion) that I promised David."

But how are you going to know how to renew your soul if you don't spend time reading the covenant, if you don't spend time meditating on the covenant God has with you? The renewal, restoration and revival of your soul precedes understanding the ways of the Lord and the operation of the mind of Christ within you. Renewal even precedes the operation of divine health and healing for your body. John the Apostle said, **I wish above all else that you may prosper and be in health, even as your soul prospers** (3 John 2 NKJV). John understood that spiritual development precedes natural development.

The Glory of God — In You

Before we look at verses four and five of Isaiah 55, let's remind ourselves to whom these verses are addressed. God is still talking to those who are:

- thirsty for the things of God,

- those who have come and bought the wine of the Spirit, and the milk of the Word without price,

- and those who have eaten it.

He is talking to those who:

- listen to the voice of the Spirit,

- who have inclined their ear to hear Him,

- who hear with understanding,

- and who are part of the everlasting covenant made with David according to the mercies of God.

It is important we understand to whom Scripture is addressed. Not every Scripture can be accurately claimed by any believer. With the above in mind, let's take a look at verses four and five:

> **Indeed I have given him as a witness to the people, a leader and commander for the people. Surely you shall call a nation you do not know, and nations who do not know you shall run to you, because of the Lord your God, and the Holy One of Israel; for He has glorified you.**
>
> **Isaiah 55:4-5 NKJV**

Whole chapters could be written on each of these verses, but notice that the new covenant believer, with a heart after God and a hunger for more of His ways, fulfills all of the requirements for those to whom this is addressed. Also, notice at the end of verse five that this believer has been glorified by Jesus. This is key.

This verse refers to new covenant believers, who have His glory inside their reborn spirits. Listen to God's words: **. . . and the Holy One of Israel; for He has glorified you.** Now, God did not glorify anyone under the old covenant. It just didn't happen. They saw His glory. Moses saw His glory on Mount Sinai. Abraham saw His glory when, as a fiery torch, the glory passed between the covenant pieces.

Moses and Abraham were witnesses. They saw God's glory manifested. The Shekinah glory was present in the holy of holies in the tabernacle. At various times the Shekinah glory was present in the temple of Solomon, sometimes so strongly that the priests could no longer stand up and minister. But the priests themselves were not glorified.

The Shekinah glory of God means one thing — the manifested presence of Almighty God. The day that Jesus died and new creation reality came into existence, the veil between the holy of holies and the people was rent in two. That was the day it became possible for the glory of God to indwell human beings. When you were born again, you literally became a portable ark of the covenant, and the glory of God is now resident inside of you. Your spirit man is glorified!

If you have been baptized in the Holy Spirit with the evidence of speaking in tongues, then you have a miraculous manifestation of His presence right on your tongue. It is proof of His glory residing in little old you.

Do you comprehend, dear one, that you have moved into a realm beyond that of any of the heros of the Old

Testament? Your body may not be glorified, and your soul may still have a long way to travel on its road to full renewal, but the glory of Almighty God is inhabiting your spirit. Awesome, isn't it?

Prepared for Revelation

The higher thoughts of the Lord include you! They have since the foundations of the world. Through your new birth in Jesus you are being prepared for His revelations by the indwelling Holy Spirit. You have the capacity to receive the revelation of God's higher thoughts via the mind of Christ, which you possess because your spirit was glorified by the indwelling of the Holy Spirit. As a believer you are the most unique and powerful creature ever to walk the face of the earth. Jesus is our prototype, and it is to His image that we are being progressively conformed.

Now, as we get ready to move on to another chapter, I have another question for you. Are you cooperating with that work of renewal, restoration and revival that God wants to do in you, or are you resisting it?

Of course you can be a partner to the higher thoughts of God. He made you, in Christ, able to receive, contain and minister them. I think the key question is — how "in Christ" do you want to be?

If your answer is more "in Christ" than you are now, then read on. You are making progress already.

4
Higher Thoughts — Part 2

4

Higher Thoughts
Part 2

He was a round, crusty, old prophet and what hair he had left was white. He seemed slightly impatient most of the time, and when asked a question, he would first look in the eyes of the asker, as if to measure the honesty of the inquiry. His answers were rarely what one expected, but always insightful beyond the anticipated. He seemed to have some special link with the God he so diligently served.

Children seemed to love him most, and the feeling was mutual, for he found in their eyes an honesty purer than their parents'. His blue eyes, deep set in a jowly face, would twinkle with mischief as the children told him their secrets. Each Sunday after the service the little ones would come to the front of the sanctuary and get their hugs, tell their stories and hear his advice.

Their parents, while friendly enough, would wonder what it was in this teddy bear of a man who drew children to him. They had seen his ocean blue eyes turn slate gray when he was confronted with deceit or sedition in his flock. They knew him to be ruthless in confronting sin, yet compassionate to the point of weeping over pain, sorrow and repentance.

His answers were beyond the wisdom anyone could predict, and they knew he walked in closer communion with God than they did, and they were jealous. One of the children put it best, "It is like talking with God," she said, and it was.

He was odd. But they were drawn to him, without knowing why, without wanting to be and with a hope that, somehow, in the presence of his fire, they could be made pure again. He was a prophet!

He could be quite patient with the genuinely inquiring and abrupt with the self-serving. It was to him I put my question one afternoon over lunch.

"How do you know if it is really the voice of God you are hearing?" I asked.

His eyes measured mine for one long moment, and then a slight smile crossed his face and twinkled out his eyes. The inquiry was sincere, and I knew I would get my answer.

"Two ways have always worked for me," he said. "First, God is a lot smarter than I am and His answers are almost always something I never would have thought of. You know, higher thoughts. He has a viewpoint I don't have. And He knows the hearts of men. My wisdom is like me looking through a knothole in a construction fence and seeing just one part of the project, but His wisdom looks over the top of the fence and sees the whole thing.

"Second, God will always give me Scripture to back up what He says. He doesn't say anything that isn't in accordance with His Word. The Bible is filled with God's higher thoughts, and I have learned to recognize His voice by recognizing how He thinks. Jesus thinks the same way the Father does, and we have the mind of Christ!"

The Very Thing

As one of my staff members finished relating the above true story to me, I was struck with the realization that the old prophet, in his own way, had hit upon the very thing I have been saying for as long as I have been teaching this message.

46

Learning to hear the voice of God within you is easy if you will take the time and trouble to develop a relationship with the speaker. Learning to develop the mind of Christ in you works along the same lines: first, develop a relationship with the Lord, with Whose mind you have been blessed.

I can hear some of you now as you read this, "Don't tell me it all boils down to relationship?" Yes, it does!

The very thing that keeps most believers from developing the mind of Christ in themselves is that they approach it as though it were some sort of comic book super power rather than an instrument in the hand of the Lord. They want to retain control of the how, why, when and purpose. It doesn't work that way. God is calling you to a much higher level of intimacy with Him. After all, aren't we, the Church, called the Bride of Christ? And that means surrender.

Think about this for a moment. We are smart enough in our human marriage relationships to know that we must be authentically who we really are and that we must also allow the other person to be who he or she really is if the marriage is going to succeed. There can be no pretending, no masks, no role playing. Transparency and authenticity are what counts.

Don't you suppose that God is at least as smart as we are? He is going to require as much of us as we do of each other. We can no more successfully pretend or put on a mask in front of God than we could in front of our spouse. What makes us think we can fool God?

What kind of pretending and mask wearing do we do? What are we trying to hide?

We put masks over our sin. We pretend it isn't there or that it isn't so bad, not really. We try to hide our nakedness before Him just as Adam and Eve did and for the same reason — fear. We are fearful of being discovered to be less than perfect, of being rejected if we admit to our condition. Nothing could be further from the truth. God wants us to run to Him when we sin, not away from Him.

In the passage we have been studying, Isaiah 55, God doesn't mince any words on the subject:

> **Seek the Lord while He may be found, call upon Him while He is near.**
>
> **Let the wicked forsake his way, and the unrighteous man his thoughts; let him return to the Lord, and He will have mercy on him; and to our God, for He will abundantly pardon.**
>
> **Isaiah 55:6,7 NKJV**

Did you know that the above passage is not talking about the unsaved? It is talking about believers who have lost their first love. God is talking about the believer who has become wicked in his ways and the unrighteous man in his thoughts. He didn't say, "Let the wicked forsake his wicked thoughts." He said, **Let the wicked forsake his way** (v. 7). Why? Because those ways are at cross purposes with the plan of God. They get in the way of the relationship God wants to have with us.

Here is how we know they are believers. The end of the verse says, **Let him return to the Lord** (v. 7). That means they are coming back. Backslidden, cold, out of fellowship believers are coming back. And notice that God doesn't say He will hit them all with a big stick. No, He says, **He will have mercy on him** (v. 7). For whom? For the person who has wandered off. And God doesn't stop there either, **He will abundantly pardon** (v. 7).

This higher thought concerning believers returning to the Lord is also found in the New Testament in 1 John 1:9 AMP, **If we confess our sins (wicked ways and our unrighteous thoughts), He is faithful and just to forgive us of our sins and to cleanse us from all unrighteousness.** God is going to forgive our sinful ways and cleanse us from our unrighteous thoughts, continually pardoning us and letting the blood of Jesus cleanse us of sin all the time — if we will return to Him. Our Heavenly Father wants to forgive us. He wants to have mercy on us. He wants us not only to be in right relationship with Him, but also to be in intimate fellowship with Him.

A Picture for Us

Verse eight of Isaiah 55 begins with a thought that seems to be unrelated, but it isn't. It is an illustration of how and why God's thoughts are higher than ours and how we can tap into them.

> **For My thoughts are not your thoughts, nor are your ways My ways, says the Lord.**
>
> **For as the heavens are higher than the earth, so are My ways higher than your ways, and My thoughts than your thoughts.**
>
> **For as the rain comes down, and the snow from heaven, and do not return there, but water the earth, and make it bring forth and bud, that it may give seed to the sower and bread to the eater,**
>
> **so shall My word be that goes forth from My mouth; it shall not return to Me void, but it shall accomplish what I please, and it shall prosper in the thing for which I sent it.**
>
> **Isaiah 55:8-11 NKJV**

What a picture! God is speaking. He is showing us two things. First, that His thoughts and ways are higher than ours, and second, that we can participate in the process of establishing those thoughts and ways in our lives. We participate with Almighty God when we return His word to Him. Until it is returned, it lies fallow, but when we speak it or act it back to Him, the power in His Word activates itself on our behalf. Then it accomplishes the purpose for which God sent it.

But we don't just fall into thinking God's thoughts and walking in His ways. We don't just naturally speak His

Word back to Him to complete the cycle of power. Thinking, patterning our ways and speaking His word are all contrary to the natural mind and its inclinations. What it is like is the supernatural. But God's thoughts and ways are not what the natural man likes to hook up with. It has always been so. We have to have our minds renewed in order to be able to function in God's way.

In his letter to the Corinthian church, Paul said that the righteous ways of God are folly to the natural (carnal) mind. He said if the philosophers and wise men of this age could have understood the plan of God through their philosophy and their arguing, they already would have; but now, he said, there is no way the natural mind of man will ever understand the mind of Christ or God's thoughts.

> **But the natural man does not receive the things of the Spirit of God, for they are foolishness to him; nor can he know them, because they are spiritually discerned.**

> **1 Corinthians 2:14 NKJV**

"How will we to be able to do it then, Louise?" Well, dear one, God never tells you to do something without telling you how to get it done.

Remember we talked about God's Word not returning to Him void? We are the ones who do the returning. Words must be spoken or declared in order to move in the spiritual dimension. God needs someone to speak His words back to Him in order for them to be returned. He needs a pray-er. He needs an intercessor confessing the Word of God into a situation. He needs His Word declared to give the Holy Spirit an opportunity to convict hearts. He needs His Word spoken in the earth in order for it to return to Him. It isn't our responsibility to get it up to Him, just to speak it out in the earth. Are you and your mouth available for God to use to establish His covenant in the earth?

Look and See — Hear and Understand

If we had a think tank of four or five hundred of the best minds in the world we wouldn't even make a dent in God's higher thoughts.

We put little men into a metal tube, shoot them as high as we can and they circle the earth in orbit, and we think we have done such a big thing. We shoot them into a bigger orbit, and they land on the Moon. We send cameras and telescopes into orbit to find out things about space, and we don't even have the foggiest idea how big space is, let alone what might be beyond it. Our highest thoughts are minuscule compared to God's lowest thoughts.

Let's look at some of the accounts we have about God's higher thoughts in the Word.

Who would have ever thought a little band of Israelites, raised as slaves for 400 years, who didn't have a gun to their name, who didn't have a stick of dynamite or any modern weapon in their whole population, could overturn the government of the most powerful nation in the world? But they did — because of God's higher thoughts and ways!

Here is another of God's plans which must have seemed like foolishness personified to the Israelites. God's way was to have them walk in circles around the heavily walled city of Jericho blowing trumpets and rams' horns and not saying anything for a week. Then everybody was to shout at once, and the walls would fall down flat so they could go in and conquer the city. Right, sure!

Man's natural knowledge laughs at such a preposterous situation. The soldiers and people of Jericho laughed, too. Some of the guards hollered down to the Israelites, but they didn't say a word. No cheers to encourage themselves, no positive talk, no nothing — just silence. What a crazy way to fight a war!

Jericho's walls were thick enough at the top for chariots to race around on. The pounding of the Israeli feet wasn't going to jar those walls off their foundations, and a few priests tooting on some rams' horns weren't going to vibrate the walls down either. But God's higher thoughts and God's higher ways had them marching silently day after day, and at the end, with a shout the walls all fell down flat. It is a fact!

Look at Gideon. He starts out with a mighty force of thirty-two thousand men and ends up with 300 men who didn't know anything about fighting. What do they take to war? A candle and a water pitcher. And God's higher thoughts confused the enemy so badly that they killed each other. And 300 men came home with the victory over many thousands.

Noah built the ark in the middle of a land-locked area with no way to get the ship to water and no history of it ever having rained enough to float the thing where it sat. Yet, for over a hundred years he labored at God's appointed task, providing a higher way according to God's higher thought for him and his family, and it saved their lives!

Just as He did for these men of faith, God has created a walk in the Spirit for you. Your reborn spirit was created to be supernatural. If you will allow yourself to become subject to God's higher thoughts, when you march around your walls in obedience to Him, your walls will come down, too.

Your Faith Project

Some time ago I spoke at a minister's conference in another state, and the pastor of one church told me the following story:

"One day, right before we were getting ready to start a big building program, a homeless man came to us asking to do some work for food. We fed him and sent him out to pull weeds in the front of the church. Pretty soon a van pulled up, and a man with an iron pipe got out, came over to the homeless man and started beating him up for no apparent reason. The homeless man fought back and ended up beating his assailant half to death. The police came to break it up.

"Several days later, I was sitting in my study and I got a notice from the courts saying that I was being sued by the assailant, the guy in the van, because the homeless man beat him up, and I, acting on behalf of the church, had told the homeless man, who wasn't even part of our church, to go cut weeds. I was being sued for over three million dollars! First I laughed, then I cried. The whole thing felt crazy.

"I made some phone calls, and things got even crazier. The lawyers told me that juries like to think that the poor little guy who got beat up ought to get compensated, even though he started the fight, because the church was so big and could afford it. Besides, they figured, we had liability insurance, didn't we? Well, yes we did, but not for anywhere near that amount of coverage. I could just see all the money we were going to use in the building program going to this unjust cause.

"I began to pray. I began to confess the Word, God's higher thoughts, over the situation. *No weapon formed against [me] shall prosper, and every tongue which rises against [me] in judgment [I] shall condemn. This is the heritage of the servants of the Lord* (Isa. 54:17.) I dug into the Bible and got several verses that I could stand on and spoke those out my mouth regularly.

"My spirit man was saying, 'You can't lose. You will win!' But my mind was saying, 'Who are you kidding? You have already lost, sucker.' Day after day I would battle like this, but the only thing I would let come out my mouth was my confession of the Word. I would not speak negatively.

"We went to court. It dragged on for several days while this man, our accuser, brought in his wife and all his little kids. They got on the stand and told how poor they were and how having their husband and daddy hurt so badly that he couldn't work was such a hardship on them. I was even feeling sorry for them myself.

"When the jury left the courtroom to deliberate, my lawyer told me I didn't have a prayer against this man. But I knew that was exactly what we had. He would say, 'Don't get your hopes up,' and I would say, *No weapon formed against [this church] shall prosper* (Isa. 54:17).

"When the jury finally came in, they found in favor of the church, saying we had nothing to do with it. God's higher thoughts had become my higher thoughts through the mind of Christ, and faith was my victory."

And You?

Do you have a faith project? Maybe your project is a wayward son or daughter, an unbelieving spouse, a health issue or impossible finances. Our church is believing for more classroom space. Whatever your challenge is, the principles are the same. You get the mind of Christ by finding out what the Word says on the subject. This will reveal God's higher ways. Believe those thoughts on purpose in spite of what your natural mind says. Declare the Word, specific Scriptures that are expressive of those thoughts, over your situation. Water that word-seed with prayer, praise and worship, wait with patience for the harvest and then reap diligently when your harvest comes.

It may be months that you speak the Word, pray the Word and water your seed by praying in the Holy Spirit. Remember, Satan knows that when you get hold of this truth, he is in for a fight. So he erects strongholds to keep your faith project from being manifested in the natural. But if you will stay firm in your faith walk, believing the Word over circumstances, believing the Word of His higher thoughts over your own thoughts, you are going to win every single time.

Recently I asked my congregation, "How many of you, in the last five years, have had a major faith project come into manifestation?" Nearly half the people raised their hands. Are you standing for a faith project now? If you won't waiver, it will come to pass. It will absolutely come to pass! God is not a liar. His Word will not return to Him void, but it will prosper in the thing for which it was sent.

When God's Word is active in your life and you are operating with the mind of Christ, you can't help but prosper. Everywhere you put the Word to work in your life, it will prosper. It will accomplish. But it has to come out your mouth. It has to return to Him.

That is the part that seems to be so tough — for people to begin to confess God's Word over their own thoughts and into their situations. Can you imagine somebody who is sick and racked with pain in their body going around saying, "I am healed by the stripes of Jesus. Pain, you are a liar. I choose not to believe you. I choose to believe the Word which says that my body is healed." Now, does that sound like natural thinking? Of course not!

Natural thinking says, "Quick, give me a couple of aspirin! Give me a couch and two pillows and shut up." That is the natural mind, not the mind of Christ.

When you look at your checkbook balance and see nothing but zeros, it isn't natural to stand in faith, to lay your hands on that checkbook and say, "I am not moved by what I see. I see the Word working for me. I see prosperity coming, for Your Word shall prosper this checkbook." You are operating in the mind of Christ when you confess the truth of the Word over a situation instead of the facts your mind understands. Meanwhile, your natural mind is going nuts, wanting to know how much you have left on your MasterCard line. Do you know what I am saying? I have been there too, so I know what I am talking about. Dear one, the Word is God's higher thoughts and higher ways!

And it is nuts to your natural mind when your kids are doing everything in the world — wrecking cars, smoking dope and getting into all the trouble they can find — and you walk around confessing, "My children are disciples of the Lord, taught of God. My children shall come from a far land, and they will come into the courts of righteousness. The seed of the righteous shall be delivered. I and my household shall be saved." But you and your spirit can operate in the mind of Christ even when your natural mind is saying, "Yeah, but God, it looks like they are all going to hell."

You and your wife are practically at the divorce court. She won't talk to you. "Talk to my lawyer" is all you hear. And you are going around saying, "I and my household walk in peace. No weapon formed against me shall prosper, and God, you know divorce is a weapon." If you can shut down your natural mind, you will win every time. The mind of Christ is far more powerful than your natural mind.

Your husband is struggling with drugs, alcohol, anger, lust or you because of your desire for more of God. Or maybe it is your wife. I want to tell you, if you will get into the Word and begin to call those things that be not as though they were, you will create a spiritual hedge of thorns around that rebellious soul. If they can't make you mad, you have them licked. If you won't fight with them, they don't know what to do because they are eaten up with conviction. Learn to fight in the spiritual realm, and you will have victory in the natural. God's Word will not return to Him void. It will prosper in the thing for which it was sent.

But it takes time. Will you wait for the Word to work? Are you willing to let God operate on the basis of His Word in your life according to His timetable? Will you surrender control to Him? Of your life? Of your plans? Of your dreams? It is hard; I have been there. I know. But to walk in God's higher ways, you must surrender to His higher thoughts. That is why you have the mind of Christ — to enable you to operate in God's higher thoughts according to the mysteries of God. You can operate with the mind of Christ, but not without cost.

Will you spend the time it takes?

Will you make the effort it requires?

Will you trust God's plan?

5
The Great Plan

5

The Great Plan

Do you know what the Devil is more afraid of than anything else in your life? Humility. True humility. When you and I humble ourselves under the mighty hand of God, the Devil is scared to death of our humility. Why? Because it was the humility of Jesus, Who humbled Himself even unto death, that defeated the Devil in his attempt to overthrow Almighty God.

Satan knew exactly Whom Jesus was and the scope of His power. He was prepared for a direct confrontation to battle the majesty of His glory, but not for a humble entrance, in a stable, in an obscure town, at an inconvenient time. The humility of Jesus put Satan off balance, and he never recovered. Satan used the rulers of the world to do his bidding, but their twisted minds and the Devil's together were never wise enough to figure out God's great plan until it was too late. In fact, the Bible says in 1 Corinthians 2:7,8 NKJV:

> But we speak the wisdom of God in a mystery, the hidden wisdom which God ordained before the ages for our glory,
>
> which none of the rulers of this age knew; for had they known, they would not have crucified the Lord of glory.

The extent of our humility before the Lord is the extent to which God makes Himself responsible for our success. When we are willing to lay down everything and follow Jesus one hundred percent, Satan has no weapon with which to come against us, and the Father will do everything necessary to cause us to triumph over every attack.

How many times in Scripture have we seen this principle illustrated?

- **But He who is greatest among you shall be your servant** (Matt. 23:11 NKJV).

- **He who finds his life will lose it, and he who loses his life for My sake will find it** (Matt. 10:39 NKJV).

- **Therefore humble yourselves under the mighty hand of God, that He may exalt you in due time** (1 Pet. 5:6 NKJV).

Do you "get it," dear one? God's plan is for you to follow the example of Christ. For you to be fully "in Christ" means to take on the humility of Christ so that you might have the victory of Christ. God is ready to assume full responsibility for the life completely yielded to Him.

Jesus humbled Himself even to death on the cross to make you His own. He said that anyone who wouldn't take up his cross and follow Him wasn't worthy of Him. For years I wondered what He meant by my cross. I heard dozens of teachings and sermons on what He meant, but finally I "got it" by revelation.

The cross we must bear is one of humility, for like Jesus, the only way God can fully use us is for us to humble ourselves. Rest assured, you will be asked to humble yourself in certain areas of your life, your plans, your pursuits and to become obedient to what God desires to do through you. If you won't pick up that cross of humility and lay down your own life's ambitions, He can't flow His life through you to others. That clogged condition is unfruitful and unworthy of the sacrifice Jesus made for you.

All Saints Come This Way

The disciples themselves were no different than you are, nor was any less required of them. Peter, who walked on water, who had the revelation of Jesus as the Messiah, who wanted the chief place among the disciples, got puffed up and bragged that no matter what the circumstances were, he would never deny Jesus. Well, you know the story. On the night of Jesus' betrayal, before the rooster crowed, Peter denied Jesus not once, but three times. The man who thought his ministry would be the greatest of all the disciples was thoroughly humbled.

Having realized it wasn't his energy, ability or zeal that God needed, but rather his availability and humility, Peter received his Lord's forgiveness and commission on the shore of the Sea of Galilee. As he walked in that humility a few months later, people brought the sick out into the streets where Peter might pass by so that if his shadow might fall on them, they would be healed.

By this point, Peter is not looking for a glorious ministry for himself. He is continually pointing people to Jesus. He would say to those who asked him by what power or name he healed a lame man:

> **Let it be known to you all, and to all the people of Israel, that by the name of Jesus Christ of Nazareth, whom you crucified, whom God raised from the dead, by Him this man stands here before you whole.**
> **Acts 4:10** NKJV

Quite a change, isn't it? And yet it was this very change, this putting on of humility, which made Peter useful to the Master. Jesus clothes us with robes of righteousness purchased by His own blood because of His humility. We clothe ourselves in humility to be worthy of Him.

Paul went through the same process. All puffed up in his religious pride, he was struck blind for three days and required to empty himself of all his religious bigotry toward the Christians. Imagine devoting your life to a cause only to find out you were totally wrong! To an intellectual like Paul there could be no greater humiliation.

Paul's intellectual pedigree was unequaled. He could have preached in any of several languages and mesmerized listeners with his eloquence, his education and his anointing. In fact, he would later hold whole stadiums spellbound, but not with any of his own abilities. He said:

> For Christ . . . sent me out not to baptize but to [evangelize by] preaching the glad tidings (the Gospel), and that not with verbal eloquence, lest the cross of Christ should be deprived of force and emptied of its power and rendered vain.
>
> **1 Corinthians 1:17 AMP**

I want to tell you, he could have preached the cross with more eloquence than the greatest orators of his day, of which there were many, but he said, "I will not deprive it of its force."

Under the anointing of the Holy Spirit Paul didn't debate; he declared the cross of Jesus. He didn't reason; he gave them the reality of their plight and God's plan for their redemption through the cross of Jesus. Understand, to the scholarly mind of that day and this, reasoned arguments, lengthy debates and intellectual presentations were the order of the day in the philosophical/theological arena. Your proposition was made, and then everyone would debate it, each giving his arguments in turn. Truth was supposedly determined by who won the debate. Paul, in contrast, simply declared the truth of the cross of Jesus without submitting the concept for debate. He declared it to be truth, period! You could take it or leave it, your choice, but you couldn't reason it away.

Foundations of Power

Where did such power come from? Its foundation came from his own humility in view of the work of Jesus on the cross in his behalf. We must look at the cross, not at our own difficulties, needs, abilities, talents or ministries. Let's stop trying to sugarcoat ourselves and the message of the cross to make it acceptable to the world. The world needs to accept the cross as it is and to be humbled by it themselves.

In our society today it is the simple, powerful message of the cross that is transforming a generation of rebellious kids. No fancy words, no slick promotional gimmicks, no smooth oratory works on them. Just the power of the cross! They recognize the real thing.

Preachers to youth all over the country are just "puttin' it out there" in all its simplicity and saying, "Guys, this Man Jesus hung on this cross and took all your sin, took all your disease, took all your care in His own body and He died for you. And if you can identify with that and know that He became your substitute, that He went to Hades in your place and conquered death for you, that when He arose, it was so you could have eternal life with Him and believe in Him so that you could have peace with God and His power for your life."

God's highest thought was the plan of salvation, the birth, teaching, death on a cross and resurrection of Jesus. That is how He showed the folly of this world. You cannot reason your own way to the foot of the cross of Jesus Christ. There is one way, and that is God's higher way. We all have to come to the foot of the cross and be washed in the blood of the spotless Lamb of God.

> **For when the world with all its earthly wisdom failed to perceive and recognize and know God by means of its own philosophy, God in His wisdom was pleased through the foolishness of preaching . . . to save those who believed.**
> **1 Corinthians 1:21 AMP**

And that is what the cross is to the New Age movement — a stumbling block and a rock of offense. That is what it is to satanism and humanism as well. It takes humility to accept Jesus as Lord and Saviour and take yourself off the throne of your heart. But all saints must come through the gate of humility. Peter, Paul, John — there are no exceptions — not even you and I.

A Mystery to Satan

The plan of God was a total mystery to Satan. But to those who are called, whether Jew or Gentile, Jesus Christ is the Power of God and the Wisdom of God, God's highest thought. It was the highest thought of the universe when the Trinity sat down before the foundations of the earth were laid and planned out Jesus' coming in the form of a man.

It would be an incarnation that would bring redemption from sin and, upon His return to the Father, make Jesus the baptizer in the Holy Spirit — the same Holy Spirit Who would not only inhabit man as His temple at the time of receiving Jesus as Lord, but also would empower man to do the works of Christ. Man would be born again and become a new creation and, thereby, be reconciled to his creator God.

This highest thought took place even before the fall of the first Adam. In the mind of God the second Adam, Jesus, was already slain, before the earth was formed, that we might be reconciled to our loving Father God.

You, beloved, are the reason behind God's highest thought. His love for you motivated the whole of it, and Jesus' love for you motivated Him to come and die in your place. The Holy Spirit's love motivated Him to come and dwell in your corrupted earthen vessel of a body. You are precious to God! It is His great plan that you be conformed to the image of Jesus — in fellowship, in power and in love.

Humility is the door. Do you possess the courage to walk through it? On the other side you will be in the company of Peter, Paul and thousands of others who were used mightily by God.

Circumstances Can't Win

What we so often cringe from are our circumstances. But when you are operating in the mind of Christ, even circumstances will bow their knee. Did you know that when Paul wrote his letter to the Philippian church, he was in prison? He was imprisoned by the strongest government in the known world, the Romans. He recognized that when he was at the end of himself, he was his strongest in Christ's power.

In his letter he is essentially saying: "The Roman government does not have the right to put me to death. I will choose when I go. And I will stay here as long as it is my will and God's will, and I am accomplishing the purpose for which He has called me." You talk about a higher thought! Paul had prayed that into his spirit man. Remember he said, **I speak with tongues more than you all** (1 Cor. 14:18 NKJV). He was operating in the mind of Christ.

Some might say he was really at the mercy of those who had him in chains. He got the soldier or prisoner chained to him born again! If you study it out in history, you will find that they were the seeds of the martyrs that came along in great numbers later. Through the third century, Christians could trace their spiritual lineage back to those who wore chains with Paul in prison. Circumstances are merely a tool in the hands of God. The mind of Christ is a total mystery to Satan, but nothing is a surprise to God — nothing!

Holy Ghost Detour

At this point, when I was teaching these lessons in my home church, the Lord took me a way other than I originally thought the teaching would go. By that same inspiration, I am going to go that way here for you as well. We may cover some ground that you know very well, but maybe you haven't realized how powerful and important it is to you.

Praying in the Holy Spirit is every bit as supernatural as raising the dead! That's right. In spite of the fact that for the last several years we have had some wonderful teaching in the Body of Christ on praying in the Spirit, most Spirit-filled Christians have no idea of the importance and benefit of praying in tongues. It has become common and, therefore, not exercised as it was intended to be, nor for the purposes for which it was intended.

The Apostle Paul was the vessel God used to write the vast majority of the doctrine that we rely upon today. He authored over half of the books of the New Testament. He was without peer in spiritual insight, doctrinal understanding and revelation. Yet Paul made only one claim of difference between himself and other believers. He said, **I thank my God I speak with tongues more than you all** (1 Cor. 14:18 NKJV).

Yes, there is a connection, and I want to build that bridge for you now. In 1 Corinthians 14 Paul had some interesting things to say about speaking in tongues:

> **He who speaks in a tongue does not speak to men but to God, for no one understands him; however, in the spirit he speaks mysteries.**
>
> **He who speaks in a tongue edifies himself.**
>
> **What is the conclusion then? I will pray with the spirit, and I will also pray with the understanding. I will sing with the spirit, and I will also sing with the understanding.**
>
> **1 Corinthians 14:2,4a,15** NKJV

You have a key to the power of Almighty God! He gave you a language to use when you communicate with Him. Verse two above says that when you are speaking in tongues, you aren't speaking to men; you are speaking to God.

Now, let's take this one step at a time, together. Why do you suppose God would give you a special, private language just to communicate with Him?

Is it like a security phone which scrambles your message so no one can know what is being said except the receiver who has an unscrambler? In a sense, yes, but it is more.

Is it so there can be instant access to the Father for urgent needs and priority situations? Yes, but it is more.

Is it so we can have control over this facet of communication with the Father? Yes.

You see, in all the other verbal gifts of the Holy Spirit (tongues for the assembly, interpretation and prophesy) the control rests with the Holy Spirit as He wills. But we choose when to exercise our private prayer language.

Well, Louise, what is the benefit of my having that control? I will answer that in a moment, but first, let's understand what is actually happening in the spiritual dimension when we are praying or singing in the Spirit. You have to know what is going on in order to grasp the full impact of why your control over this element of your Christian life is so powerfully transforming.

As Paul pointed out in verse two above, when we exercise this gift, we are speaking mysteries to God. Why would God have us speak mysteries to Him? I mean, they can't be mysteries to Him; He already knows everything there is to know. But they are mysteries to us and to Satan. That is important. Think about this. If you could figure out the higher thoughts of God, the mysteries, without the mind of Christ then so could the Devil. God is not going to have His mysteries revealed to His enemy.

Actually, what happens in the spiritual dimension when you pray in the Spirit is that those mysteries resident in the mind of Christ, which is in you, are being spoken out of your spirit to God. This results in two extremely important things that can have tremendous impact on your life.

First, we know that faith comes by hearing (or more accurately, understanding) and hearing by the Word of God. Well, when you are speaking mysteries in a language you don't understand, you certainly don't "hear" them and, therefore, can't exercise any faith toward them. So what is the point? The point is that God can understand those mysteries because they are His to begin with, and He mixes His faith with them to make manifest in your life the very higher thoughts you were speaking.

Second, we know that God supplies seed to the sower and bread for the eater. Now, the sower of the Word in this case is you. You are the one speaking the mysteries of God to Him in the Spirit. Therefore, God's Word is returning to Him. God then returns it back to you in the form of a harvest of revelation, in which He desires you to operate. Why revelation? Because like produces like. What you were sowing by the Spirit was pure Word; therefore, what you will harvest is pure Word straight from God. That is revelation.

In other words, when you pray in the Spirit, God is able to activate His faith to manifest the reality of that mystery in your life and give you a harvest of additional revelation you can sow back to Him for more edification. What a circle of unending blessings! You pray mysteries so God can bless you with revelation, so you can pray more mysteries, so He can bless you again with more revelation.

When the Lord took me another way that time I was teaching the lessons in my home church than I thought the teaching would go, this is the way I saw what happens when you pray in tongues!

Edify, Edify, Edify

Did you know that Jude commanded us to pray in tongues? (Jude 20.) He said the result would be that we would be built up in our faith. With all the above happening, it is no wonder!

The word Paul used to describe the result of the praying and blessing in our lives is edification. To be edified means to be built up. We get our English word *edifice*, or large building, from it. Can you see how God has designed this tool to bring forth the reality of His higher thoughts in your life? You and I need to pray in tongues! It is one of God's master tools for conforming us into the image of Christ.

I would be remiss if I didn't point out that praying in the Spirit can also be a form of intercession, and when it is so used, the edification benefits accrue to the one for whom you are interceding.

You can edify yourself any day, any time, any place, and the way is by praying or singing in the Holy Spirit. In my church at home we laugh about the "Hour of Power in the Shower," but it is a good example of the places and times you can use to edify yourself. Another good one is in the grocery store. Claim the Scripture in Deuteronomy 28:5 which says your basket is blessed in the store, and then pray in tongues as you go up and down those aisles! One staff member told me she does far better doing that than clipping coupons.

Now you can pray in tongues, getting quiet before the Lord. Then, either by the mind of Christ operating in revelation or interpretation, you can receive His higher thoughts for that day, that week, that counseling session, that job interview, that relationship, whatever you need and even things you didn't know you needed. You have that kind of power residing on the inside of you, but some people (not you, of course) are so stubborn or prideful or lazy, they won't pray in tongues enough to get God's higher thoughts. If you will be a self-edifier, then God can move you into other areas where you can minister.

But you are in charge of your own edification. You decide how built-up you become spiritually. Loved one, I lay at your feet the responsibility for building yourself up in your most holy faith by praying in the Spirit in the car, in the store, in the shower, on walks, in the kitchen, in your bedroom and in your work place. You don't have to be loud. God hears you even when you whisper.

Then do you know what will happen? As you begin to speak God's Word out your mouth by the Spirit, the power of that Word will begin to work its transforming power in your life and the lives of those for whom you pray. I don't care if you have rebellious kids. I don't care if you have bills stacked clear up to your chin. I don't care if your hope has all but vanished. I have experienced all those things and more, and God has delivered me from all of them by the power of His Word in exactly the way I am describing to you. It works!

All you need for today is one hour of God's higher thoughts, and you can be a success in every area of your life. With the mind of Christ in operation in you, He can give you more wisdom and insight in one hour than you can get through a whole lifetime of natural thinking.

God is no respecter of persons. The same mind of Christ that operated in Paul operates in you, But, Paul prayed in tongues more. We have some catching up to do, don't we?

6
The Easy Yoke

6

The Easy Yoke

"It isn't supposed to be this hard. Is it?"

She had asked the final question. After more than an hour of pouring out her troubles and problems, she had come, finally, to the root of her frustration.

"What is wrong with me?"

Another final question came from a huge bear of a man who was weeping openly in his frustration at not being able to make things work in his family the way he knew they should.

"How could God possibly use someone like me?"

The teen's despair was evident as he quietly asked the question that sat like a stone in the bottom of his heart. He was "no good" in his own eyes. How could he ever be any good in God's eyes?

Have you asked yourself one or more of these questions? I have. Believe me, I know the frustration and despair of thinking there must be some basic truth about life that I don't understand or that there must be something seriously wrong or defective with me or that perhaps God couldn't use me because of my past mistakes.

You, too? Well, welcome to the club. If you will look up as we pass through the clubhouse doors, you can see the sign that reads, "The Called of God." What? Yes, that is right! If you have ever asked any of those questions, or a hundred more just like them, you are precisely the one for whom the Lord has been looking. You are eminently qualified for what Jesus had in mind when He said, **Take My yoke upon you and learn from Me . . . for My yoke is easy and My burden is light** (Matt. 11:29,30).

Answers to Final Questions

My heart ached for all three of these precious people of God. They felt they were at the end of their ropes with no knot to hang on to. All they had, in their minds, were questions they couldn't answer.

But there are answers to those questions! I know because I found them, and they work! The root problem all three of those people faced was that they thought the only solution available to them was through their own control of their situation.

The woman's frustration turned out to be caused by her substituting her own expectations for God's. No, it wasn't supposed to be that hard. When she learned to rest in and trust a loving Father, she had the peace and joy she longed for.

The bear of a man couldn't make his family work properly due to a misunderstanding of his role as husband. There wasn't anything wrong with him, except his fear that if he didn't stay in control, everything would fall apart. As soon as he began to surrender his need to control to the Lord, his relationships with his loved ones began to heal.

The teenager who was consumed with guilt learned that his doubt that God could forgive and use him was rooted in his lack of self-forgiveness, which he was using as an excuse to avoid changing his lifestyle. In other words, he used self-pity as a control mechanism to allow himself to continue sinning. Of course God could forgive and could use even him. Look at the work God did with Paul. When he faced the fact that God had already forgiven him in the finished work of Jesus and that all he had to do was accept it for himself, he had his choice, peace or continued torment, clearly before him. His already accomplished redemption led him to a new freedom in Jesus.

One Step Further

In this chapter I want to show you from the Word how you can take everything we have talked about, put it all together and make it work. I know the world talks about getting your act together, but in spite of hundreds of books, tapes, videos and seminars, the truth is, they don't know how.

Would you like to find out, once and for all, how it is done? Have you gone as far as you could go and then known there was just one more step between you and final victory, but you didn't know what that step was? Wouldn't you like to know what that one last step is that would bring your life to a place of continual victory?

In the Church there is a lot of talk about the Holy Spirit. We talk about the need to be born again by the Spirit of God. We talk about the need to be filled with the Spirit or baptized in the Spirit. We need the fruit of the Spirit and the gifts of the Spirit. But there is one very important aspect about the ministry of the Holy Spirit that is neglected today, the need to be *led by* the Spirit of God.

After you have been born again and baptized with the Spirit, after you are bearing the fruit of the Spirit and operating in His gifts, there is one more step you must take. You must be willing to be led by the Holy Spirit daily. If you are not willing, your frustrations will mount up until those final questions plague your life, and they will continue to plague you until you surrender to His leadership.

The Lord is not looking for broken lives; He is looking for surrendered lives. Frequently, because of our stubbornness, He has to wait until a person's life is broken before they are willing to surrender it to Jesus. But that isn't the Lord's first choice.

A man in my church has worked with the Seeing Eye Dogs program as a trainer. He tells me that training the dogs is often easier than training their owners. "Some people," he said, "who are stone blind, will still insist on leading themselves even though they have a well-trained animal to lead them. They have no peace at all. Constant worry steals all their joy."

Sometimes the Lord must think that we are like those blind people. We are so stubborn. We insist that we be allowed to continue controlling things ourselves. We say we want to be led, but we reserve the right to say where. It doesn't work that way, dear one.

The one step further you must take is the step of total surrender to the daily leadership of the Holy Spirit in your life.

One lady in my church said that when she did this, she saw a vision of her answering her door to find a man standing on her front porch. He was dressed very nicely and carrying two big suitcases. The man didn't speak, but she knew He was the Holy Spirit. Then she asked Him how long He was planning to visit. He answered her, "I am not here for a visit. I am moving in."

To whatever extent you will yield to the Holy Spirit, He will, to that same extent, lead you in your daily life. He is a gentleman. He will not enter any area of your life uninvited. But He will masterfully guide you when given the place of leadership in your life that God has designed for Him to have. After all, He is your access to the mind of Christ.

The Word at Work

Throughout this book we have been learning from the 55th chapter of Isaiah. Let's look now at verses 12 and 13 NKJV:

> For you shall go out with joy, and be led out with peace; the mountains and the hills shall break forth into singing before you, and all the trees of the field shall clap their hands.

> Instead of the thorn shall come up the cypress tree, and instead of the brier shall come up the myrtle tree; and it shall be to the Lord for a name, for an everlasting sign that shall not be cut off.

Remember, this chapter is written to the children of Israel when they were in bondage, captives in Babylon. When the Lord speaks of going out in verse 12, He is referring to going out from bondage. And when He speaks of being led forth, He is referring to the journey to their land of promise.

We have the same opportunities. Whatever bondage has ensnared you, you can be free from it. Whatever journey you must take, you can have His direction. God does not show favoritism. What He has done for others, He will do for you. Let's take a closer look at exactly how this passage of Scripture bears on what we are learning about developing the mind of Christ in you.

Remember that we said the plan of God was that we be conformed to the image of His dear Son, Jesus? Well, Jesus was never successfully held in bondage during His entire life, death or ministry. Not even the Devil's ultimate weapon, death, could hold Him. It can't hold us either!

Therefore, if not even his ultimate weapon can have final victory over us, why do we sit still and allow him to win smaller victories? He has no bondage from which we cannot break free. Yes, it takes great strength sometimes, but the Word says that we shall go out with joy, and the joy of the Lord is our strength. (Isa. 55:12; Neh. 8:10.)

Now, if you will look again at Isaiah 55:12, you will notice that it is, in fact, that same joy which causes you to break out of the bondage of your captivity. Sin can hold you captive, make no mistake about it, but the joy of the Lord will set you free.

Look also at what leads you toward the promises of God — His peace. When you are led by peace you won't make a mistake. That's right! The peace of God, the Bible says, will garrison our heart around (Phil. 4:7 AMP), and we will know whether to turn right or to turn left. We will know whether to buy or to sell. We will know whether to invest or not to invest. We will know exactly whether to plant or whether to reap. We will know exactly what we are supposed to do when we are led by the Spirit because the Holy Spirit will not hurry you or put you into a corner where you have to make a decision overnight. You will be led forth by peace.

When the Word of God is working, that is, you are speaking it back to Him so that He can return it to you in a harvest of revelation, you will break out of bondages with the joy of the Lord, and you will be led forth to the promises of God by His peace in your heart. Read that sentence again — it's important.

You see, dear one, when you are operating with the mind of Christ in the higher thoughts of God, you will see and understand things others won't. Then the joy and confidence that comes from those revelations will cause you to rise up in faith to defeat every attack against you, overcome every obstacle in front of you and achieve every goal ahead of you.

When you are consistently led by the Spirit of God, His peace surrounds you, and you operate in a place of spiritual authority that cannot be assailed successfully.

When the Word of God is at work, you cannot be defeated!

Singing Mountains and Clapping Trees

Sounds odd, doesn't it? I mean, mountains don't sing. Trees don't clap. Or do they? No, I am not getting weird on you. But I do know there is a finer line between what we call the natural and the supernatural than most people think. Consider this: everything that exists in the natural realm was created with words. It stands to reason, then, that these natural things would respond to their creative force —words spoken in authority. Jesus spoke words, and the wind, the waves, a fig tree and a dead man all obeyed Him. Why? Because He spoke them with authority but, more importantly, because He was operating in the higher thoughts of God.

When we operate in those same higher thoughts, because we have developed the mind of Christ in us, then our words will have the same impact as Jesus' words did. The point made in Isaiah 55:12 NKJV is to illustrate the fact that the natural is controlled by the supernatural:

The mountains and the hills shall break forth into singing before you, and all the trees of the field shall clap their hands.

God is more than able to alter the unalterable, to change the unchangeable — even when it looks impossible — and to deliver you across your personal Red Sea when it seems you are trapped.

When you tap into the supernatural thoughts of God and begin to understand the supernatural ways of God, the natural forces of your life will join behind you in praise.

You can speak to the mountain of problems, the hills of adversity and the trees of your own forest of confusion, and when you are operating with the mind of Christ, they will respond to the Word of God spoken out of your mouth. Your mountains will come down, your hills will sing and the trees will clap their hands for joy! Circumstances tremble and shake in the face of the power of the Word of Almighty God, their creator. Wouldn't you?

Weeding Out Thorns and Briers

Now look at verse 13.

> **Instead of the thorn shall come up the cypress tree, and instead of the brier shall come up the myrtle tree.**
> **Isaiah 55:13a NKJV**

First of all, let's notice that these cypress trees and myrtle trees came up without being planted. Thorns and briers should have come up because their seeds were in the ground. But instead, wonderful trees sprang up and flourished. Why?

Because, when you are operating in God's higher thoughts, the natural will always bow to the supernatural. The supernatural is natural to God.

Have you, in your rebellion, ever planted some thorns and briers? Are you still, even today, getting stuck by some of them? Did you ever wish you could go back and dig up those hurtful seeds? Maybe you have even prayed for a crop failure. Unfortunately, anything with thorns always seems to grow faster and more stubbornly than anything else, doesn't it?

But there is a way to have cypress trees come up where you have planted thorns and myrtle trees where briers should be. Here is how — with your mouth. Yes, your mouth! Your confession over those seeds will determine what you will see when those seeds are full grown. Let me illustrate with a story I can laugh about now, but it sure wasn't funny at the time.

I made a dumb mistake. Yes, me. I made a big mistake on a business deal. I took a partner, and each of us invested $25,000. We got nothing in return. In fact, the whole thing turned out to be a hoax. Well, I went before God and said,

"God, I thought I heard your voice. I really listened, but I guess I just missed You." I was pretty upset about it, crying and feeling sorry for myself. Do you know what God said to me?

"Quit sniveling, quit whining. Get up, because when your heart is right and you repent of a mistake, I will prosper that mistake."

"Oh, my goodness," I said, "I repent right now! I ask you to forgive me. I made a mistake! Now prosper me that $25,000 quickly!"

And do you know what happened? Nothing, right away. But for the next three years that money came in month by month for me to pay off that debt. I learned more through that experience about trusting God day by day and month by month for that huge amount to come in than I would have if God had dropped the whole $25,000 right out of heaven into my hand. Besides, if He had, I would probably have gone out the next week and done another dumb thing.

God prospers His Word! He values it even above His name. He will even prosper your mistakes if your heart is right.

I can just hear some of you now as you read this. You are saying, "Well, that might work with money, but what about this problem I married?" Let me tell you, God will even prosper that! If you will get your confession lined up with the Word, God will change that nagging spouse, that rebellious child or that impossible circumstance. You may have planted thorns and briars, but you will rest in the shade of cypress and myrtle trees. It will happen!

God's Word will prosper in the thing for which it was sent. Just don't expect it to happen overnight. Now let me ask you. How long does it take a crop to mature in the field?

One rain? Two? Jesus addressed this when He talked about the man who put his seed in the ground and then slept and rose night and day while the seed sprouts and grows and increases, he knows not how. (Mark 4:26,27.)

Two different Greek words for *time* in the Bible are *chronos* and *kairos*. One means time as we use it, but the other means seasons. In our microwave society we tend to confuse them all the time. We want God's seasons to be merely time, but He doesn't work that way. There is a right season for everything, and God's timing is perfect. Remember, His sense of timing is not changed by our anxiety or nervousness.

Operating in the mind of Christ includes learning to be at peace with the seasons of God's timing. The longer I operate in the higher thoughts of God, the easier it gets for me to relax and let things take their God-ordained course. You can rest assured that if you are in the center of God's will for your life, you are in the season you are supposed to be in, and God's timing is working toward your exaltation.

That's right — your exaltation. God desires to exalt you, to have you flow in His peace, His joy and His wisdom. In fact He even says He wants your ability to function in the supernatural arena of His higher thoughts to be so commonplace in your life that it will cause people to know that you belong to Him.

> **And it shall be to the Lord for a name, for an everlasting sign that shall not be cut off.**
>
> **Isaiah 55:13b**

Through His prophet Isaiah, God is expressing His desire to see natural circumstances changed into supernatural blessings: mountains, hills, trees, thorns and briers are all transformed by the power of the Word. Further, these signs are to be an everlasting sign of His working in our lives through the working of His Word. Throughout history, and still today, it is the presence of the truly miraculous that validates the presence of God and authenticates His ministers. The presence of the supernatural in your life can become as normal as breathing if you are willing to surrender totally to Him and wear His yoke.

The Light and Easy Yoke

Let's go back to verse 12, where Isaiah talks about going out with joy and being led forth by peace. There is a very basic truth here we must consider if we are to understand how to flow with the mind of Christ and to operate in God's higher thoughts.

If we go out and are led forth, then we must be going somewhere. And how we go determines the quality of the journey. Simple, isn't it? We can only operate in the joy and peace of God if we are going somewhere spiritually. If we aren't maturing spiritually, our joy and peace are going to be diminished.

Jesus invites us to take His yoke upon us. Why would He do that if it weren't for our benefit? Think with me for a moment. What are the purposes of a yoke?

- It helps distribute the weight of a burden
- It directs the wearer where to go
- It concentrates energy for maximum effect
- It controls difficult behavior
- It fosters teamwork and cooperation
- It is a sign of ownership and value
- It keeps the wearer humble
- It is useful for training

I don't know about you, but I want all of those things from my relationship with Jesus. I want to have Him share my burdens, direct my steps, use me mightily, control my difficult behavior, teach me teamwork, value me as His possession, teach me humility and train me well. How about you? It is a difficult thing to lay down pride and set self aside, but if we are going to wear His yoke, His easy yoke, it must be done.

Still, the basic truth about the necessity of movement and spiritual growth is very important. If we are going to wear His yoke and be led by peace to our land of promise, we must think about what a trip like that will require. Twenty gallons of gas and air in the tires isn't enough. Neither is being born again and Holy Ghost baptized. It is a journey on which you *must be led*.

I think it is only fair, however, to tell you what the journey will require of you. Some of these things you will have in full supply when the journey starts, most you will have only in partial supply, and some you may have none of. All will be required, however, so you will have to learn to fill your supplies as you go. Here is the list. Your journey out of your bondage, being led by the peace of God, in His timing and seasons will require:

Patience. You won't make it the first day, or even the second.

Purpose. You must know the purpose for which you have been redeemed.

Planning. Count the cost and plan well. Spend your time wisely.

Prayer. This is the fundamental key. Pray in the spirit every day.

Provision. No expedition goes on a journey without food, water and salt.

Persistence. No matter what. You can't be defeated if you will never give up.

Priorities. Keep these straight and stay focused and everything else will fall in line.

Sounds like a tough job, doesn't it? If you are like me when I first began to understand what a job it was to keep myself on track, the first thing I wanted to know was, "Where can I get some help on this?" Well, that is what the next chapter is all about —getting help from the source God has provided.

Are you ready to shoulder your pack and move out?

Are you ready to take His yoke upon you and learn?

Then let's press on and learn about getting the support, encouragement and help we need.

7
The Greatest Show in Glory

The Greatest Show in Glory

7

The Greatest Show in Glory

P. T. Barnum was wrong!

The circus is *not* the greatest show on earth —the Church is. It is the showplace of the glory of God today! God's glory far outshines anything Barnum & Bailey could cram into a three-ring big top.

But the Church is changing. It is maturing, becoming more disciplined and more bold. It is being pressed by the world, and it will continue to be pressed until Jesus returns. Why? So that it can be conformed to the image of Jesus.

> Now it shall come to pass in the latter days that the mountain of the Lord's house shall be established on the top of the mountains, and shall be exalted above the hills; and all nations shall flow into it.
>
> Isaiah 2:2 NKJV

Do you know what this is saying to us? In the last days the Lord's house, the church, is going to take a higher place than anything else in your life. It will be more important than even your job. Everything in your life will flow toward the Lord's house, be scheduled around it and be prioritized below it. It will become the focal point of your life.

There is a cataclysmic event coming. I don't know what it is going to be, but it is going to drive people back to the Lord's house. People keep asking me if it is going to be Ezekiel 38 and 39. I don't know, but when the event happens, it will establish the church on the highest mountain.

If I were to take a survey of every reader of this book, I would probably find at least half a dozen good reasons why you love to come to church. But the days are coming when it will be far, far more important to you than it is now. You will place it on the highest mountain of your life.

Look at verse three of that same chapter: **Many people shall come and say, "Come, and let us go."** Do you know why? Because it is a place of refuge. It is a place of safety and security.

There are dark days ahead financially in the United States of America. There are dark days ahead socially in our land. Dark days lie ahead of us in the area of our health. If we just knew the truth about everything, we would be utterly shocked.

A medical doctor from Washington, D.C. came to one of my meetings in Virginia, and a group of us went out for a bite to eat after the meeting. He was explaining some things to us about health issues in our country. He said, "If the general public knew the extent of the AIDS epidemic in the United States, there would be total pandemonium."

I want to tell you, if your church is important to you now, you just wait a few years or maybe even just a few months. I wouldn't be surprised to see churches that are full of the life and the power of God having services every day.

> **Many people shall come and say, "Come, and let us go up to the mountain of the Lord, to the house of the God of Jacob; He will teach us His ways, and we shall walk in His paths." For out of Zion shall go forth the law, and the word of the Lord from Jerusalem.**
>
> **Isaiah 2:3**

Put this verse with the verse that says, **The just shall live by faith** (Rom. 1:17), and you begin to get a picture of how things are going to be. The church will become the centerpiece of the believer's life because that is where the Word of God is preached. And since faith comes by hearing, and hearing by the Word, people will be coming to the church to find out how to survive in the perilous times ahead of us. Only those who are operating in the Mind of Christ and God's higher thoughts are going to see clearly in those days.

Welcome to the Show

There is something supernatural happening now. Pay close attention because today one of God's higher thoughts is corporate gatherings. You can hear God's voice for yourself in your kitchen, you can hear His voice in your car, in the grocery store and on the job, and you should be hearing His voice in all those places. But there is something supernatural that happens when we come together to praise and worship and hear the Word of God.

There is a corporate anointing that comes in, and it rests upon all of us. I don't have the whole counsel of God. Neither do your pastors, your elders or your parents, but when we come together in a corporate gathering, we come closer as a Body to having His whole counsel than anybody does separately.

The glory of God is shining out and showing forth in the corporate gatherings of His Body around the world as never before.

Now, I am not down playing your own private time with God. We have spent a considerable amount of time right here is this book emphasizing our need for just such times in order to develop the hearing ears on the inside of you that will be sensitive to the mind of Christ within you. But to give you the balanced approach I need to spend some time in this chapter giving you an understanding of our need for the church in our lives. We need both private and corporate times of fellowship with God. In corporate meetings there is a corporate anointing with supernatural power that is different from what you experience by yourself. God's power is intensified by the number in the meeting when we are together.

Three Rings of Fellowship

First, your Church must be like your family to you. If they aren't, if they are dead and cold, you need to get to another fellowship that teaches the Word of God with power.

Second, you must be connected to your Church. It won't do you any good in the days to come to slip in the back after the service starts and leave before it ends so that you don't have to talk to all those people. You need to be connected through smaller groups within your fellowship as well. Go to your cell group or special interest group. Get connected!

Third, you must be committed to the spiritual well-being of the other members of your fellowship. Where can you lend a hand? Where could you make a difference? What can you supply to your local Body to help it grow?

I suggest, dear one, that you learn to love God's house before you desperately need it. I suggest you learn to love God's people before they are all you have left. You may have noticed that in the world that nobody's word means anything anymore. You may have noticed that everybody is only looking out for himself, "for number one" as they put it. That is not family, and that is not God's plan. God's higher thought is for corporate gatherings. We must come together in the Lord's house.

No More Lone Rangers

We all must submit ourselves one to another. We must also submit our ministries to a local Church if we are going to flow in a full anointing. If you think that you can sit in your living room and prophesy to two people and that you can get all your spiritual food from television, you are nuts. You can't do it. The days of the Lone Ranger ministries are over! A Lone Ranger ministry operates unprotected and will get shot down by the enemy.

Think about it. You can't cut off an arm from the body and expect that arm to live. It will shrivel and die. It will stink because it is flesh. If you don't stay hooked into divine life and the supernatural nourishment of the local Church where God has planted you, you will become a mess. Notice that I said where God has planted you. Make sure that where you are attending is where *God* wants you to be, not where your flesh feels the most comfortable.

Did you know the word "church" isn't even in the Old Testament? It is a concept born in the mind of God and birthed by the lips of Jesus. We want to put a lot of blame on men for the Church, but the Church was God's idea. He set it up. He ordained its Godly government, set forth the qualifications for leadership and established the precepts of discipline. Now, men and women can get their ideas into it and foul it up. But God's idea is still right, and somehow He manages to work around and through all the mess we make and achieve His purposes through this Body of His called the Church.

You need a local Church Body to help keep you on track. But that Body needs you, too. You have gifts vital to the life of that Body. Don't think the local Church is there just to keep you in line. Your gifts, appropriately ministered, will help your Church stay on its track as well.

The Birth of the Church

In the book of Acts, the Church was birthed in the fire of the Holy Spirit and, like a newborn babe, she cried out. She cried out in tongues. The first words ever uttered by this newborn creation of Jesus were in tongues. That alone ought to tell us something about the importance in our lives of speaking in tongues.

Further, the Church was birthed in a corporate gathering! There were one hundred and twenty charter members, every one of them in unity, when suddenly a sound like a mighty wind enveloped them, and tongues of fire rested upon them. God put the sign of the seal of the new covenant upon that member of our Body which causes us to be born again by our confession — the tongue. And it happened at a corporate gathering! It doesn't matter how individualistic you may be, or how independent you want to be from the Church. The Church was born at a corporate gathering, and when we go out of this world in the rapture, we are going as a corporate gathering. Face it. God's plan is the local Church. His commandment to us is not to forsake the assembling of ourselves together.

You and Your Church

One of God's higher thoughts is His Body in corporate gatherings. Jesus is not going to take just this one and that one. When the trumpet sounds, the Church, the corporate gathering, the Body of the Lord Jesus Christ, is going to rise from this earth and meet the Head of the Church in the air!

So if you think you can isolate yourself now, wake up! You need the Church now more than ever. The local Church is where God is concentrating His focus in our generation. If you are not in a local Church, you will be missing out on a large portion of what the Holy Spirit is doing, and you will be missing out on the effect the corporate gathering has on developing the mind of Christ in you.

You might just as well get used to corporate gatherings; besides, they teach us how to walk in love with our brothers and sisters. Around the throne of God there is going to be a corporate gathering such as none of us has ever seen before. It will be the greatest service you can imagine. Abraham,

Moses, Paul, Noah, John the Baptist, Jeremiah, Elijah, Enoch — they will all be there. (I am going to ask Enoch, "Where did you go?") And you will be there, too.

Those of you who are faithful to your corporate gathering have a responsibility to those who aren't faithful. You need to love them and pray for them and stir them up.

Don't make it the responsibility just of the pastoral staff. Don't just make it the job just of the board of elders or deacons or administrative staff. It is the job of everyone who is a part of a corporate gathering. It is your responsibility to warn, to encourage and to get those people participating in the life flow of the Holy Spirit in your local Church. The job of the leadership is to be your trainers so that you can do the work of the ministry. Be constantly expanding your circle of friends in your Church. Don't just say, "Us four and no more."

The local Church is the greatest thing on this earth. Jesus left the Church as His Body. These corporate gatherings are important, as are camps and conventions, but it is the local Church where covenant is installed, where covenant is enforced. We are responsible to walk out our covenant with each other, in love, just as much as we are responsible to walk out our covenant with God Almighty!

A Great Cloud of Witnesses

The Amplified Bible renders the first verse of chapter 12 of the book of Hebrews like this:

> **Therefore then, since we are surrounded by so great a cloud of witnesses [who have borne testimony to the Truth], let us strip off and throw aside every encumbrance (unnecessary weight) and that sin which so readily (deftly and cleverly) clings to and entangles us, and let us run with patient endurance and steady and active persistence the appointed course of the race that is set before us.**

Do you see it? You have to stay in the Body of Christ! That means you have to stay in Church. Find one that is family for you, where you can get connected and stay committed. Allow God to plant you there. Then let your roots grow deep in the soil of covenant relationships there. The mind of Christ will flourish in that environment, and you and that local Body will reap the harvest.

Why is being involved in Church so important? Because the Church is where much-needed discipline and correction can take place. Now, I know none of us likes correction, but we all need it. God can correct you when you are alone, but most of the real correction comes by the anointed word of someone. Your spirit receives it as *rhema*, and you begin to line yourself up with the Word.

Verse five of Hebrews 12 in the Amplified tells us: **Do not think lightly or scorn to submit to the correction and discipline of the Lord.** We all, as the whole Body of Christ, need the correction that comes from the Holy Spirit. Our traditions block the power of the Word of God in our lives, and only through the mind of Christ operating in us can we see and understand things as Jesus does. We need to have our course corrected sometimes. I know I do.

23.6 Cubic Feet Off Course

Don't ever get the idea that because someone is in full-time ministry, they are immune from God's corrections. Our corrections are sometimes even sharper and harder than yours might be. The Lord demands that His leadership walk in covenant, and He will see to it that we do.

A few years ago we were taking an offering for Mike and Ethel Keyes, missionaries to the Philippines whom we support. I said from the pulpit that I loved them so much, and being in covenant with them, I was as concerned about their needs as I would be about my own son Bruce and his wife or any of my other children.

It was only a couple of days later that the Lord said, "That was a lie." Well, I thought, I wanted it to be true.

"Couldn't we just call it an untruth?" I asked.

"No," was His simple answer. So, I had to repent to Him and to my whole congregation.

I have tried to keep my heart so pure with these kinds of things. That is why it is always a joy for me when I work through something I can share with you because I know what you are working through.

Well, the story behind the story goes like this. We had been furnishing Mike and Ethel's place for them so that when they were here, they would have a nice home. They needed a refrigerator, and we were delighted when we found an excellent buy on a six month old 23.6 cubic foot frost-free GE Americana with ice and water in the front door. It was almond colored with stay-clean textured doors.

It was everything I had hoped it would be, and they wanted about half of what it would have been worth new. "I'll take it," I said.

Then my flesh got into the act. I thought, well, Bruce and Kathy's refrigerator at home is white, and we need a white one for Mike and Ethel's house. So, I'll get the new one and put it in Bruce and Kathy's place and take their 17-year-old white one and move it to Mike and Ethel's. After all, they are only going to be using the place just a couple of months a year anyway.

I justified this all the way back to the church. In fact, I even gave directions to accomplish the moving of the old white refrigerator over to Mike and Ethel's house. Then the Lord let me know the real truth of what I was doing. "You are not walking covenant with Mike and Ethel as you would with Bruce and Kathy, and as you said you were from the pulpit," He said.

Then I knew the truth. If it had been my own children, I would have kept my old white refrigerator and gladly given them the new one.

So we took the new refrigerator to Mike and Ethel's house, and I paid for it. That almond refrigerator is sitting in their house, and I have sown that money in good soil. It doesn't matter to me whether they are home two months out of the year or two days. The little hook of selfishness that the enemy had worked into me God worked out of me because I was willing to walk covenant faithfully and accept His course correction, and that correction came in a corporate gathering.

After I made that decision and spoke it out of my mouth — and I made that decision so firm the Devil just took off in a hot run — it yielded the peaceable fruit of righteousness. You see, what happened to me when I yielded to that discipline and that correction and received the peaceable fruits of righteousness in my heart was that I had a peace about what I had finally done. That peace garrisoned around me and Satan hasn't been able to fool me with that tactic since.

Learning the Love Walk

Let me be the first to tell you, if you haven't found out for yourself already, it is tough to walk the covenant of love in corporate gatherings. We have every mix of personalities you can imagine in the Body of Christ. We have gentle, abrasive, sweet, slick, loving, assertive, submissive and just plain cantankerous, not to mention totally fearful, deeply angry and passionately devoted. We are a wonderful cross section of the humanity Jesus died to save. Seems like some of each ended up in my Church. Yours, too?

Well, I am not going to quit coming to church just because someone acts in a way that I don't like. I am not their judge; Jesus is. Just because someone, maybe even you, acts ugly in church is no reason for me to quit. It is reason for me to pray and to love more. My job is to strive to love everybody in the Body of Christ. It isn't going to happen by next Tuesday. It is an ongoing process. It is a daily, progressive walk in covenant.

So if you know God has planted you in your church — stay there till He transplants you. You don't have the right to quit just because Sister So-and-So acted ugly last week. Let's grow up! The Church is family. My guess is you don't always get along perfectly with every person in your earthly family. Everyone seems to have at least one relative that he just has to love anyway. You don't disown your whole family just because you don't get along with one member of it. Our Church family should be the same way. God looks on the heart, not on how "spiritual" you are. Let's get real with each other as well as with the Lord.

Another part of learning to walk in love is learning to confront. We hate to confront, don't we? I have to tell you, I was one of the most mealy-mouthed, nonconfrontive church members you ever knew. I would gripe to my friends or go home and cry. I hated confrontation. But I was determined to walk in covenant and in love so, you guessed it, God changed me from my old nonconfrontive self into someone who can't stand for anything to be in the way of my relationship with another believer.

If I sense that something is wrong, I am going to come right up in the person's face and ask, "What is wrong? Do you have an offense with me? Because if you do, I want you to forgive me. If I did something, I didn't know it. Will you forgive me?" You wouldn't believe the reactions I have received doing this. I get some of the stupidest answers.

I did this not long ago to someone I had worked long and hard to establish in our church. I sat right in front of her, looked right in her big brown eyes and said, "I don't like this wall between us. Whatever I have done, I want you to forgive me." She nearly dropped her teeth. I said, "We have had such a great relationship and such a wonderful fellowship, if I have done something to offend you in word or deed, I ask you to forgive me. If you will tell me what it is, I will make it right."

Well, she couldn't speak for a few minutes, and when she finally found her voice, she said, "Oh, I don't feel any wall." I said, "Don't lie. You have a spirit, and you are sensitive, too." Finally, she said, "Well, that's true." There was a long pause, and then it all came out. It was some silly little thing (isn't it always), and we worked it out. Now we are both happier and enjoying our fellowship once again. Satan cannot defeat the force of love. The love walk is unconquerable!

Walking in love, walking in covenant, is God's "tough love." And sometimes you have to confront with love. I will tell you, when you do, it knocks all the barriers out of the way. They will either get mad at you, or they will cry and forgive you. They are already mad at you anyway, so what have you got to lose?

We all need an attitude adjustment and further revelation concerning our individual relationship with our local church and our corporate gatherings. Cell groups are fine, prayer groups are fine and small groups are good, but they must simply be a part of the vine of life of the corporate local church.

Do me a favor, would you? Read that last paragraph over again to yourself slowly, and let the truth of it sink into your spirit. God woke me up at 4:00 am and had me write that paragraph down for you, exactly as you see it. It is important. It is important to you!

Make this confession out loud with me:

Lord Jesus, forgive me for taking so lightly your corporate gatherings. Forgive me for slighting the local church. Jesus, if you will teach me, I will be more faithful. I will be more loving. I will be more committed to my brothers and sisters. Give me a vision, Lord. Give me a revelation of my place in the local church. Let me be responsible for those around me because I care. I love them. Teach me, Jesus, to be a vital part of Your universal Body and of this corporate gathering. Amen.

The Grand Finale

Jesus designed His Church very thoughtfully. The Body of Christ is designed along the same lines as the human body. Just as human blood is the life of the body, so is the blood of Jesus, that which gives us life in Him. Just as we are built around a framework of bones, a skeleton, so is His Body, the Church, built around a framework of God's grace, without which we could not exist or stand upright before Him. A system of muscles, tendons and nerves provide the structures for functional use to our bodies, just as faith, patience, endurance and hope do for the Body of Christ. And finally, covering the whole body is the largest part of all, the skin. So, too, in the Body of Christ, love covers all.

You cannot develop the mind of Christ without learning to walk in love! It is impossible. The very badge which marks our identity is our love one for another. We cannot escape the need, the desire, the necessity and the command to love. It is something about which we have no choice and from which we have no retreat. Love! The mind of Christ can be understood only from the standpoint of His love for His Church.

I am not talking about some syrupy, outward, show of affection toward fellow church folks. I am talking about decided, committed, family-type agape love; the giving kind of love; the not-counting-the-cost kind of love; the self-sacrificing kind of love; the Jesus kind of love which is unconditional, forgiving, restoring and rebuilding; and the kind of love that saved you and me from the direction we were headed, that pulled us up out of the pit of Satan's clutches, that redeemed us from our mortal enemy, who had defeated us and taken us captive at his will.

That kind of love is uncompromised not situational, compassionate not critical, caring not condemning, patient not picky, and grateful not gossipy. Do you have that kind of love for your brother and sister in Christ? Understand, dear one, if you truly desire to develop the mind of Christ in you and walk in God's higher thoughts, then that kind of love is precisely what Jesus will be developing in you. It must be so in order for you to be conformed into His image and fulfill the great plan of God for His beloved creation — you.

One Day Soon

One day soon we shall be sitting around the table at the Marriage Supper of the Lamb. We will see old friends, loved ones, family members, yes, and even former enemies. The food and drink will be the very finest in all the universe and the table setting something to behold. Perhaps we will eat from plates made of sapphires and use forks made from crystal clear gold. There will be rejoicing such as we have never known as we, the Bride of Christ, feast with our husband, Jesus.

Perhaps Jesus will rise from the head of the table and tap His water glass made of diamonds for attention. Then, when all has grown still, He will speak to each one of us. "With desire have I desired to eat this supper with you, for you are My bride, redeemed by My blood, beloved of My father and yours, and you are, for all ages to come, throughout all eternity — My Church."

Louise Brock is the founder of Faith Community Church in Tucson, Arizona. Following in the footsteps of her father and mother, she has dedicated her life to ministering the uncompromised Word of God to the Body of Christ. Louise now travels the nation and the world teaching the insights and revelations with which the Lord has blessed her.  Untiring and gracious almost to a fault, she serves a full schedule of ministry engagements every year. This book is a serving of some of the fruit of her first decade of ministry. Enjoy!

For a complete list of tapes and books
by Louise Brock, write:

Louise Brock Ministries
Faith Community Church
2551 W. Orange Grove Road
Tucson, Arizona 85741

*Please include your prayer requests
and comments when you write.*

The Harrison House Vision

Proclaiming the truth and the power
Of the Gospel of Jesus Christ
With excellence;

Challenging Christians to
Live victoriously,
Grow spiritually,
Know God intimately.